Constructing Global
Public Goods

Constructing Global Public Goods

James C. Roberts

LEXINGTON BOOKS
Lanham • Boulder • New York • London

Published by Lexington Books
An imprint of The Rowman & Littlefield Publishing Group, Inc.
4501 Forbes Boulevard, Suite 200, Lanham, Maryland 20706
www.rowman.com

6 Tinworth Street, London SE11 5AL

British Library Cataloguing in Publication Information Available

Library of Congress Cataloging-in-Publication Data
Names: Roberts, James C., author.
Title: Constructing global public goods / James C. Roberts.
Description: Lanham, Maryland : Lexington Books, [2019] | Includes
   bibliographical references and index.
Identifiers: LCCN 2019015986 (print) | LCCN 2019017975 (ebook) | ISBN
   9781498553575 (electronic) | ISBN 9781498553568 (cloth)
   ISBN 9781498553582 (pbk)
Subjects: LCSH: Public interest--International cooperation. | Common
   good--International cooperation. | Human rights--International
   cooperation. | Security, International--International cooperation.
Classification: LCC JC330.15 (ebook) | LCC JC330.15 .R625 2019 (print) | DDC
   330.12/6--dc23
LC record available at https://lccn.loc.gov/2019015986

CONTENTS

List of Figures and Tables   vii

Acknowledgments   ix

Chapter 1   A Constructivist Approach to Global Public Goods   1

Chapter 2   Accounting for Tastes: The Social Construction of
            Utility and Preferences   13

Chapter 3   Utility, Preferences, and the Individual Public
            Goods Decision   25

Chapter 4   Leadership and the Global Monetary System   49

Chapter 5   Collective Security as a Global Public Good   67

Chapter 6   The Individual Decision to Provide Collective
            Security: Romania and the Kosovo Campaign   87

Chapter 7   Human Rights: Consensus, Norms, and Public Bads   99

Chapter 8   Identities, Utilities, and Public Goods Decisions   121

Bibliography   127

Index   145

About the Author   153

LIST OF FIGURES AND TABLES

Figure 3.1   The individual's public goods decision matrix   31

Table 3.1   The 24 permutations of the public goods
preference orderings   32

Figure 3.2   The special privileged utility model   33

Figure 3.3   The privileged utility model   35

Figure 3.4   The intermediate utility model   36

Figure 3.5   The latent utility model   37

Figure 3.6   The assurance utility model   39

Figure 3.7   The chicken utility model   39

Figure 4.1   Public goods game for monetary management—
1945 to 1958   59

Figure 4.2   Public goods game for monetary management—
1958 to 1961   60

Figure 4.3   Public goods game for monetary management—
1961 to 1971   62

Figure 4.4   Public goods game for monetary management—
1971 and beyond   64

Figure 5.1   U.S. decision to participate in the Kosovo campaign
as a threshold good   75

Figure 5.2   Canada's decision to contribute to the
Kosovo campaign   77

Figure 5.3   Greece's decision not to contribute to the
Kosovo campaign   81

Figure 6.1   The Romania-NATO normal form game   96

Figure 7.1   Bandwagon effect of consensus on human rights principles   108

Figure 7.2   Shift in utilities for a norm from stage 1 to stage 3   114

ACKNOWLEDGMENTS

This project has been a long time in the making. Although none of this material has been published before, elements of chapters 3, 4, 5, and 6 were presented at professional conferences of the International Studies Association, the Midwest Political Science Association, and the Southern Political Science Association. Funding to support this project was provided by a grant from Towson University Faculty Development and Research Committee.

Many people provided valuable ideas and advice that made this book possible. In particular, I would like to thank Philip Cerny, David Lalman, Renée Marlin-Bennett, Alison McCartney, Paul McCartney, Joe Oppenheimer, and an anonymous reviewer for their comments in person and on panels. As always, I am indebted to Nicholas Onuf and his vision of constructivism.

I would also like to thank Elaine Vaurio and Emma Roberts-Vaurio for their patience and support. This book is dedicated to them.

ONE

A Constructivist Approach to Global Public Goods

At the turn of the twenty-first century, liberal authors turned from the explanations of cooperation under anarchy of neoliberal theory to the game theoretic analysis of global public goods to explain cooperation in international relations. Two important volumes (Kaul et al. 1999 and Kaul et al. 2003), which were sponsored by the United Nations Development Programme (UNDP), provided the backbone of the literature for this new movement. It was an inspired move. By drawing on a rich history of public goods literature, analysts could at once explain why cooperation often does not occur and they could provide the conditions necessary for cooperation to occur. These explanations depended on well-known behavioral phenomena, such as free-riding, that could be modeled with simple games. Analysis of public goods is firmly rooted in neoclassical and behavioral economics. Both game theory and the assumptions of neoclassical economics were challenged by the constructivist literature in international relations, which placed the examination of global public goods in the middle of the ongoing debate between rational choice theory and constructivism. This book addresses that debate, not by trying to bring the understanding of global public goods into constructivism, but by bringing constructivism into rational choice explanations of the provision of public goods.

Nicholas Onuf characterized constructivism as "a theoretical stance whose name points up its central and distinctive claim. Social relations make people social beings; people as social beings make a whole world, and not just a world of meaning, out of their social relations" (Onuf 1997a, 7). Although constructivism has taken many paths since Onuf's initial work, its defining characteristic is the recognition that agents construct social relations and social relations also construct social agents. To bring constructivism into the rational choice explanations of the provision of public goods is to recognize that the primitive objects of rational choice theory—utility and preferences—are socially constructed. Agents participate in the provision of global public goods, not because of some artifact of their strategic interaction, but because they have socially constructed

1

preferences that give them incentives to participate. These preferences are constructed from their relations with other agents and their identities derived from historical practices and systems of rule. By understanding the social construction of preferences, strategic interaction can reveal explanations for the provision of public goods that lie hidden to the rational choice theorist who claims that preferences are given, stable, and incomparable.

Public goods dilemmas are ubiquitous at all levels of social interaction. Examples of public goods problems are legion in the literature on local, state, and national governance. Kaul et al. (1999 and 2003) provide case studies of global public goods in trade and financial regimes, climate change, preservation of cultural heritage, epidemiology, regulation of cyberspace, and many other areas. The classic response to the undersupply of public goods is for some higher authority or government to provide the public good. The problem with global public goods is, of course, that there is no effective higher authority to help provide public goods in the international system. Kaul et al. (1999) identify three "gaps" in the arrangements for providing global public goods. The jurisdictional gap refers to confusion over who may be best suited or responsible for providing public goods—civil society, national governments, or international regimes. The participation gap refers to the problems related to increasing participation in the provision of public goods at each of these levels. Finally, the incentive gap results from over reliance on official aid and formal state-to-state transfers to create incentives to participate in the provision of public goods.

Public goods are goods or services that are non-excludable and indivisible.[1] Non-excludable means that once the good or service is provided, all members of the society or group for which the good is provided may make use of it. Indivisible means that the good cannot be divided up and consumed in individual portions. That is, one agent's consumption of the good does not diminish the supply of the good available to other users. A public park is an example of a public good. Once it is created, anyone can use it (non-excludable) and one person's use of the park does not use it up. It is still available for the next user (indivisible). Although public goods are indivisible, they can be crowded. That is, the number of users does not reduce the supply but it can reduce the marginal utility of each user. For example, the crowded public park on a sunny Sunday afternoon may not be as enjoyable as the serenity of the near empty park on an early Thursday morning.

The two characteristics of goods—excludability and divisibility—create four categories of goods. Private goods are both excludable and divisible. They are classic consumer goods purchased and used by individual consumers. Club goods are excludable, perhaps through a membership or subscription fee, but cannot be used up by individual consumers. A private golf course is a club good because membership fees make access excludable but one player's use of the golf course does not diminish the supply of the course for the next player. Common pool resources are non-excludable but can be used up. A public fishery is a common pool resource because anyone can use it but the resource can be used up through over fishing. Common pool resources have risen in importance due to questions about how to manage the environment (see De Moor 2015, Faure et al. 2017, and Ostrom et al. 1994). Club goods and common pool resources are referred to as impure public goods due to their having some of the characteristics of "pure" public goods. Public goods, or pure public goods, are both non-excludable and indivisible. Services, such as lobbying for legislation, can be a public good because, once the legislation passes, all members of society benefit from the lobbying effort and the lobbying effort cannot be used up by its beneficiaries.

Non-excludability creates the dilemma in the provision of public goods and common pool resources. Consumers may be unwilling to contribute to the provision of the good because they can use the quantities of the good provided by someone else without paying for them. Public goods and common pool resources are commonly under-supplied due to this free-rider problem. Kaul et al. (1999, 3) add another set of criteria to define global public goods.

> The second criterion is that their benefits are quasi universal in terms of countries (covering more than one group of countries), people (accruing to several, preferable all, population groups), and generations (extending to both current and future generations, or at least meeting the needs of current generations without foreclosing development options for future generations).

Global public goods include foreign policies aimed at maintaining system stability, management of the global commons, the protection of human rights, and the prevention of structural violence.

RATIONAL CHOICE AND PREFERENCES FOR PUBLIC GOODS

Mancur Olson's seminal book, *The Logic of Collective Action*, framed much of the literature on public goods since it was first published in 1965. Olson explained public goods by examining three types or groups of individuals. Privileged groups succeed in providing public goods because they have individuals who receive benefits from the public goods greater than the costs. Intermediate groups have members who receive substantial benefits from the goods but not enough to warrant their individual contributions. These groups can succeed in providing the good if the group is small enough that production of the good emerges from the strategic interaction of its members. Latent groups have members whose benefits from the good are small relative to the costs. The only way to stimulate public goods production in latent groups is to offer external incentives or punishments.

Olson's book spawned a vast literature that examines variables like the size of the group, the number of repeated iterations, and the structure of the interaction between players. While these have been shown to be important variables, Olson's approach was clear. If a group contains individuals whose preferences for the public good outweigh the costs, then provision of the good is likely, but if the group's preferences for the good are small relative to the costs, then the group will just as likely fail. The one clear factor that affects the individual's choice to provide the good is the individual's utility derived from the good, relative to the good's cost. Thus, theorizing about the provision of public goods *should* start by understanding how utilities and preferences are constructed.

Rational choice theories of public goods are unlikely to take up this task because rational choice theory assumes that preferences are exogenous and rigidly stable. Another reason that existing explanations of public goods gloss over preferences is that these theories address behaviors of the group more than the preferences of the individuals. This is because they were born of neoclassical models of economies, where the actions of one or a few individuals seldom make a difference in the performance of the whole. International relations, however, often addresses the effect of the actions of a few powerful agents and because these agents act in a constantly changing political and social milieu, their preferences and motivations are not stable.

THE CONSTRUCTIVIST CRITIQUE OF RATIONAL CHOICE

The constructivist critique of rational choice has varied significantly but there are three general themes that have emerged (see Roberts 2017). The first theme is that rational choice methods are rooted in methodological individualism and exclude any significant social or structural variables. Wendt (1999, 152–153) claims that rational choice theory represents a growing trend that social explanations need micro-foundations and notes that this rejects one of the basic tenets of constructivism—that agents and structures are mutually constitutive. The second general theme in the constructivist critique is that utility is defined solely in egoistic terms that March and Olsen characterized as a logic of consequences. "Those who see actions as driven by expectations of consequences imagine that human actors choose among alternatives by evaluating their likely consequences for personal or collective objectives, conscious that other actors are doing likewise" (March and Olsen 1998, 949). March and Olsen claim, instead, that much of an agent's behavior is guided by the agent's desire to act appropriately according to the interests of institutions such as the state, or international organizations. This logic of appropriateness acknowledges the social construction of the agent's actions in the rules and norms of the social setting within which the agent acts.

The final general theme of the constructivist critique of rational choice is that rational choice theory treats preferences as exogenous objects. Rational choice theorists do not deny this claim, in fact, they use it to respond to the earlier claim that they treat utility solely egoistically.

> Rational choice theorists need to assume that people will consistently choose one bundle of goods over another. They do *not*, however, need to make any assumptions about why people prefer one bundle of goods to another. The reason why people prefer one bundle of goods to another is, in a sense, entirely irrelevant to the practice of rational choice theory and so arguments about self-interest are entirely misplaced. (Hindmoor 2006, 186; emphasis in the original)

Constructivists see this as denying the social construction of agents and structures, which is a rejection of the constructivist approach outright.

A more fundamental criticism of rational choice theory is that it is actually not a theory. It provides nothing more than a description of a process. James Morrow (1994, 17) captures this in his description of rational behavior.

> Put simply, rational behavior means choosing the best means to gain a predetermined set of ends. It is an evaluation of the consistency of choice and not of the thought process, of implementation of the fixed goals and not of the morality of those goals . . . rational actors have specified goals and a set of actions they can choose. They then choose the action that will best attain those goals . . . Rational behavior is goal directed; actors are trying to create more desired outcomes rather than less desired outcomes.

The explanation in rational choice theory is fully determined once the agent's preferences and the constraints of the situation are known (or assumed). Yet these preferences, and the utility considerations from which they are derived, are not theorized in rational choice theory.

> But how do we know what an actor's goals are? In general, we deduce actors' goals from observing their prior behavior or by experimentation. We then assume that actors will continue to pursue goals we have deduced they pursued in the past. We fix actor's preferences and allow the information they have and the situation they face to change, creating variation in their actions. (Morrow 1994, 17)

Rationality is defined in terms of maximizing utility, but the ontological primitive of utility is rarely (if ever) examined in theory. At best, utility is "revealed" through an actor's choices. This sets up the worrisome tautology that choices are based on preferences that are derived from utilities that are revealed through preferences that determine choices. Andrew Hindmoor expresses the theoretical impact of this tautology in his explanation of instrumental rationality.

> A person is rational if they are instrumentally rational, they are instrumentally rational if they have a preference-ordering which is reflexive, complete, transitive, and continuous, and if they have such a preference-ordering their rationality will manifest itself in utility maximization. (Hindmoor 2006, 184)

The *theory* of rational choice theory axiomatically establishes the conditions whereby preferences lead to choices. It does nothing to explain why actors have preferences or why they derive benefit (utility) from the outcomes of the choices. Relying on revealed preference theory, the motivations for choice are intentionally left out of the theory. Thus, rational choice theory simply provides a description of the choice process, revealing nothing about the causes of decisions.

SOCIALLY CONSTRUCTED PREFERENCES AND RATIONAL CHOICE

Actors act for a reason. Donald Davidson (1963, 686) states that an agent acts based on "desires, wantings, urges, promptings, and a great variety of moral views, aesthetic principles, economics, prejudices, social conventions, and public and private goals and values insofar as these can be interpreted as attitudes of an agent directed towards actions." To attribute action to rational choice between perceived options based on subjective utility-based preferences is not to deny the importance of rules. Rules are statements that define classes of actions from which rational agents draw inferences about which class of actions may lead to higher utility and should thereby be performed (Roberts 1997, 165). This definition places rules firmly in the context of rational choice and utility theory but it does not necessarily remove them from the realm of constructivism. The question that remains is, how are rules that provide this inference for utility formed? If preferences are themselves socially constructed then this may create a powerful tool that extends constructivism into the realm of intentionality and motivation. The linkage between constructivism and rational choice can be found in constructivism's discussion of the agent-structure problem and its attempt to address this problem in the context of identity. Constructivism views neither the individual agent nor the social structure as ontologically prior to the other. Agents and structures are co-constituted. Agents are constituted by the rules of action that define the system within which the agent exists. Those rules, and the system itself, are the result of the collected actions of agents engaged in social practices. Thus, agents create rules that construct structures that create rules that construct agents. The example that is often used is the system of sovereignty. A political agent is defined as (or granted to be) sovereign based on a complex set of rules of international law and diplomacy. Yet, that system of rules is itself constituted by a long history of practice by the very same political agents.

Constructivism addresses the agent-structure problem most effectively in its discussion of the formation of identities. As Paul Kowert stated, "If constructivism addresses any substantive problem (other than wealth or security), it is undoubtedly the way people claim for themselves, and confer on others, *identity* as agents" (2001, 268; emphasis in the original). David Campbell captures the relationship between identity and the agent-structure problem.

> Foreign policy shifts *from* a concern of relations *between* states that take place *across* ahistorical, frozen, and pregiven boundaries, *to* a concern with the *establishment of the boundaries* that constitute, at one and the same time, the 'state' and 'the international system.' Conceptualized in this way, foreign policy comes to be seen as a political practice that makes "foreign" certain events and actors. Those events and actors that come to be "foreign" through the imposition of a certain interpretation are not considered as "foreign" simply because they are situated in opposition to a pregiven social entity (the state). The construction of the "foreign" is made possible by practices that also constitute the "domestic." In other words, foreign policy is a "specific sort of *boundary-producing political performance*." (Campbell 1998, 61–62; emphasis in the original. Final quotation attributed to Ashley 1987, 51)

Thus, an identity is formed by its relationship with others. This process is deeper than merely identifying the agent as an actor within the international system. Identities do more than merely distinguish and differentiate different agents. An identity attaches interests and preferences to the agent. In her overview and critique of constructivist approaches to identity, Vendulka Kubálková (2001, 34) notes that "In simple terms, states create each other as enemies, rivals, or partners and proceed to share their interpretations of their respective identities. They also act in accordance with each other's expectations of them."[2]

Identity plays a key role in defining preferences by categorizing behaviors into practices that portray the identity. Identities are packages of rules. Agents resort to categories of rules embedded in identities to make decision making easier. Kowert (1998, 106) explicitly cites this in the context of forming identities.

Individuals are continually confronted with the problem of locating themselves, and others, in a web of social categories that periodically confront them as salient. They have limited cognitive resources to devote to this task and, as a result, must make use of certain simplifying and memory-enhancing strategies. In constructivist terms, "rules" present agents with simpler ways to interpret the world and to make choices.

In international relations, agents use identity to simplify their choices both by portraying their own identity and by ascribing identities to others. David Campbell (1998) discussed, at length, the writing and rewriting of the American identity in foreign policy texts to define the interests and preferences of a nation-state as it grew from colonies of conquest through the superpower of the Cold War. Kowert (1998) documented how the British government perceived the changing identity of the Egyptian government in the year that led up to the Suez Crisis of 1956. Messari (2001) traced the development of the Islamic "other" in the American foreign policy response to the Bosnia crisis of the early 1990s. Cooley (2006) examined the effect of how the United States established its identity in relation to so-called terrorist groups in the "War on Terrorism" that followed the 9/11 attacks. Andrei P. Tsygankov (2014) examined the role of Russian President Dmitri Medvedev in establishing Russia's identity in its foreign policy with the European Union in 2008–2010. In each of these cases, the creation of identity narrowed the action choices available to the agents and prescribed those that would most enhance utility *given the perceived or projected identity*. In the context of the constructivists' agent-structure problem, agents create rules that construct structures that create rules that construct agents. The medium for this co-constitution of agent and structure is the effect that projected or perceived identity has on the utility choices of the agents. Preferences are a form of decision rules that are constructed from the rules that create identities (see Roberts 2017). Thus, the ontological primitives of rational choice theory—utility and preferences—are no longer primitive but are caught up in the co-constitution of agents and structures that constructivism so richly describes.

GLOBAL PUBLIC GOODS IN A CONSTRUCTED WORLD

Why do agents participate in the provision of a public good? Mansur Olson (1971) offered three sufficient criteria for a group to succeed at providing the public good. The group will succeed at providing at least some quantity of the good if:

1. there are individuals within the group whose benefits from the supply of the public good exceeds their costs such that they have an incentive to provide the good, even if they are the sole provider; or
2. if the group is small enough that strategic interaction between the agents can generate otherwise unexpected outcomes; or
3. If there are selective incentives that increase the utilities of members of the groups that participate in the provision of the good.

Many scholars turned to game theory to model the public goods decision since it involves the joint actions of the individual and the rest of the collective. Some of the most illuminating models have been simple 2 x 2 variable sum games. The Prisoner's Dilemma is popular because it provides a model with a Pareto inefficient stable equilibrium that represents outcomes that replicate real-life public goods dilemmas. The game of chicken is used to replicate brinkmanship behavior in the public goods decision (see Lipnowski and Maital 1983; Taylor and Ward 1982; and Kealey and Ricketts 2014) and the assurance game is used to model situations of "sufficient complementarity" where "an agent is better off contributing when others contribute, leading to matching behavior equilibriums" (Sandler 2004, 55).

What does it mean to use a particular 2 x 2 game to model a public goods decision? By choosing a game the analyst chooses the outcome that he or she claims is a valid model of the behavior observed in public goods decisions. Choosing a game based on strategic behavior constructs the game through arbitrary relationships between costs and benefits without regard for the characteristics of the actors. The whole process takes on a tautological tone as the analyst asserts that an observed outcome is modeled by a game that is constructed to create the observed outcome. For example, the outcome of many public goods decisions is perceived to be a Pareto sub-optimal equilibrium. The Prisoner's Dilemma game is chosen to model this outcome because it is the unique game among 2 x 2 variable sum games that has a single Pareto sub-optimal equilibrium (Rapoport and Guyer, 1966). By choosing a game, however, the analyst also ascribes preference functions for the actors in the model, permitting the structure of the game to determine the preferences of the actors. This is both atheoretical and counterintuitive. Actors' preferences determine the nature of strategic games—not vice versa.

This book takes a different approach. The unknown basis for agents' utilities are examined through a variety of qualitative methods to interpret the social construction of agents' desires and beliefs—preferences—regarding outcomes of decisions about providing public goods in the international system. These preferences are then used in logical models to represent possible explanations for how global public goods are produced. The models are used to represent decision processes. They are not deterministic and are not meant to predict outcomes.

Chapter 2 discusses and provides a critique of the epistemology of rational choice theory. Rational choice theory is generally thought to be a positivist theory, yet it consistently falls short of the most basic criteria for positivism including the verification principle and the ability to generate falsifiable theory. Rational choice theory is, instead, unacknowledged scientific realism. Scientific realism seeks causal factors that explain real phenomena, even when these causal factors are unobserved or unobservable. The unobserved causal factors of rational choice theory are the utilities of the agents. Chapter two presents qualitative methods that can be used to interpret these unobserved utilities and discusses the virtues of logical models for explaining the real outcomes of public goods dilemmas using the interpretation of socially constructed utilities.

Chapter 3 presents the logical models that can be used to represent the public goods decision. These models are derived from the utility calculus an agent faces when it decides whether or not to provide a public good, not from the expected nature of the strategic interaction. These models simply represent the process of making the public goods decision. The outcomes of the decision are driven by the socially constructed utilities and preferences of the agents, not the structures of the models.

The methods for interpreting socially constructed utilities and the logical models of public goods decisions are used in chapters 4 through 7 to explore how global public goods are provided in different areas of international relations.

Chapter 4 uses the utility-based public goods model to examine United States' decisions to manage and reconstruct the global capitalist monetary system after World War II. The United States was in a unique position in 1945. Not only had the U.S. economy survived the war undamaged, it was performing at peak levels due to wartime production increases. However, none of this production could be sold on a world market near collapse. The chapter traces the development of the U.S. identity as an economic leader from the earliest stages of reconstruction through the recovery of European and Asian markets and finally to the United States pulling out of its leadership role with the end of dollar convertibility to gold in 1971. Chapter 5 uses the utility-based model of public goods to examine NATO's decision to engage in an aerial bombing campaign against Serbia in 1999.

Chapter 6 examines one state's decision to participate in the Kosovo bombing campaign in detail. Romania struggled to define its identity in the late 1990s as it emerged from communist rule and attempted to join the NATO alliance. In the midst of this struggle with its new identities, Romania was asked by NATO to participate in the Kosovo campaign by providing access to its airfields and airspace for the NATO bombers. Romania's conflicting identities as an emergent member of the Western European alliance and as a traditional friend and ally of Serbia provide an interesting case study of how identities affect utilities and preferences for providing public goods.

Chapter 7 uses the utility-based public goods model to examine international efforts to protect human rights. It begins by tracing the evolution of international consensus for human rights embodied in the Universal Declaration of Human Rights in 1948 and ends with analysis of the politics wrapped up in viewing such protections as a political nuisance and public bad by the United States during the Cold War.

The final chapter reviews the utility-based model of global public goods as a continuum of socially constructed utilities from those that strongly favor contributing to the good to utilities that view the public good as a public bad. Preferences emerge along this continuum as threshold conditions. By deriving preferences for global public goods from socially constructed utilities, Chapter 8 places the public goods decision where it belongs—in a world of social, cultural, and political circumstances rather than the tautological outcome of strategic interaction.

NOTES

1. Indivisibility is also referred to as jointness of supply and as non-rival consumption.

2. For an excellent brief overview of constructivist approaches to identity in international relations, see Messari, 2001, 228–236.

TWO

Accounting for Tastes

The Social Construction of Utility and Preferences

A UTILITY-BASED MODEL OF RATIONAL CHOICE

Preferences may motivate choice in rational choice theory, but utility defines the individual agent's preferences. Utility is an amorphous concept that has evolved over the years, especially in the economics literature. Rational choice theory derives its explanations from the observable experiences of individuals. The rationality principle, that actors act to maximize their benefits, is accepted as a nomological law. The theory asserts that there is no need to explain the source of utility that drives these nomological assumptions. However, choice can be better understood by understanding the source and nature of the utilities that define the agent's preferences. My analysis in this book asserts that an agent's utility is, in part, socially constructed and can be interpreted from the identities that the agent takes on in a given situation of choice. This leads to a utility-based rational choice model of the decision to contribute to the provision of a public good.

Jeremy Bentham (1823, 2) defined utility as the property of an action, a thought, an object, an outcome, or an event that creates satisfaction, benefit, advantage, pleasure, or good in an agent. Karl Popper defined the principle of rationality as "the assumption that the various persons or agents involved act *adequately or appropriately*; that is to say, in accordance with the situation" (Popper 1967, 359; emphasis in the original). The situation of choice encompasses all information the agent needs to achieve its ends. The situation of choice includes information on the material constraints and consequences of choice, the options for action available to the agent, the expected outcomes of those actions and their effect on the agent's utility, and the social forces that are relevant to the choice. The belief and understanding of what is appropriate to desire from the situation is affected by factors such as norms, rules, culture, history, social pressures, hierarchies, hegemonies, heteronomies, and family or clan relationships. That is, the belief and understanding of what is appropriate to desire is affected by the social structure of the situation of choice. The belief and understanding of what is appropriate to desire will vary, depending on the identity the agent takes on in the situation of choice.

To prefer an outcome is to compare it to another outcome and expect that the outcome will result in greater utility. Preferences are derived by comparing the expected effect on utility of anticipated outcomes of specific actions that are available to the agent in a choice situation. Preferences can be derived contextually or experientially. Contextually, preferences are derived from the material and social constraints of the situation that limit or expand the options for action that are available to the agent. Experientially, preferences are derived from past experiences of the agent or of other agents that communicate with the agent.

A decision model is nothing more than an attempt to represent the situation of choice. The situation of choice includes the social and idiosyncratic dimensions of utility. Since utility is unobserved or unobservable, its meaning for the agent must be interpreted rather than empirically measured. The meaning of the agent's utility can be interpreted, in part, from the identity the agent takes on in the choice situation.

It is surprising (and a bit disturbing) that rational choice theory and economic theory have so little to say about the sources of utility.[1] Milton Friedman claimed that utility should be taken as given, even though he admits that it is both a cause and a result of action. He asserts that economists have little to say about the source of utility, dismissing it as the "province of the psychologist" (Friedman 2008, 12–13).

Bentham claimed that utility is a property of an object. By the mid-nineteenth century, economists began to see utility less as a property and more as an abstraction. Jevons (1888) claimed that utility is not an intrinsic quality of objects. Instead, the value of objects varied by their scarcity and their marginal utility decreased with each additional unit obtained by the agent. In the twentieth century, Samuelson's revealed preference theory dropped off "the last vestiges of utility analysis" (Samuelson 1938, 62). Amartya Sen (1986, 61) noted that revealed preference theory "frees demand theory from the concept of preference and *a fortiori* from the concept of utility." Gary Becker claimed that many social and economic phenomena, such as the decision to marry or the use of drugs, can be modeled by an economic approach that assumes that preferences are constant and attributes outcomes to the difference between social costs and benefits. "All human behavior can be viewed as involving participants who maximize their utility from a stable set of preferences and accumulate an optimal amount of information and other inputs in a variety of markets." (Becker 1986, 119).

The evolution of thinking about utility is wrapped up with the epistemology of rational choice. Kahneman identified two types of utility in this process—experience utility and decision utility (Kahneman et al. 1997). Experience utility, associated with Bentham's utilitarian philosophy, is an expression of prior experiences of pleasure or pain. Decision utility is derived from Samuelson's revealed preference theory. Quite simply, an agent prefers A to B if the agent chooses A. Decision utility has supplanted experience utility in rational choice theory due to the difficulty of measuring sensations of pleasure and pain and because the choice itself provides everything the rational choice theorist needs to know about utility (Kahneman et al. 1997, 375). Decision utility also "expresses the positivist spirit: its resistance to subjective notions and its affection for operational definitions anchored in observables" (Kahneman and Snell 1990, 296).

Rational choice requires that preference be more than mere mechanical recordings of choice. If choice is determined by preference, then preference must also provide reasons and motivation for action that reflect the agent's utility. Hollis characterizes utility as a synthesis of desire and belief. This sets up a tension between desire-oriented sentiment and belief-oriented duty (Hollis 1987, 69). Decision utility, based on revealed preference, gives motivational priority to desire. Hollis uses the image of an old-fashioned grocer's scale with desires for and against an action loaded into the two pans and the heavier pan wins. This mechanical model requires no justification for the desires in the pans (Hollis 1987, 68). Belief, however, brings another dimension into the decision—the need to explain why the agent has a duty to act.

Hollis is not alone in identifying the dualistic nature of utility. Becker (1996, 4–5) categorizes utility into personal capital that incorporates past personal experiences that affect utility and social capital that includes the influence of the agent's social setting and structure. Malle (1999, 27) distinguishes between reasons and causes in the philosophical literature on motivation and action. Reasons are the mental states that bring about intentional action. Causes are the factors that bring about action without the mediating effect of intention. Reasons are akin to Hollis's concept of internal reasons for action generated by the "internal desires of the agent" (Hollis 1987, 74). Causes are akin to Hollis's external reasons that incorporate norms and beliefs, or as Malle puts it, "the situation factor" (Malle 1999, 47).

My approach to utility is distinctly Benthamite. I define utility as the property of an action, a thought, an object, an outcome, or an event that creates satisfaction, benefit, advantage, pleasure, or good in an agent. Utility is an unobserved or unobservable causal factor that accounts for choice. There are two dimensions to utility—an individual dimension and a social dimension. Decisions are derived from some synthesis of these dimensions.

The individual dimension of utility reflects the agent's idiosyncratic tastes that are experiential and biological responses to stimuli. I do not like to eat beef liver. I find both the flavor and the texture to be unpleasant. I like beef. I eat hamburger and steak, but I just do not like liver. I do not know why. It could be from prior experience. Being from a Midwestern American home, I was introduced to liver that was cooked very well done. I am told that liver can be quite tasty if cooked medium rare. No thanks, I do not like liver. It could be from some biochemical reaction in my taste buds. It is not from socialized learning because my parents loved liver and I suffered through many a meal as a child (maybe that's it!). My distaste for liver is not due to my religion or culture, as far as I can tell. I simply do not like liver.

Neuroscience has made tremendous progress in recent years but it cannot yet explain why people like what they like. Neuroscience can explain what happens in the brain to give us pleasure or pain in response to a stimulus. Brain studies in monkeys show that the neural processes associated with choice and reward seem to record something close to expected utility of choices made in experiments. Choices made by the subjects varied by both the level and the probability of the reward (Glimcher et al. 2005, 220). Neurons in the brain encode the elements of utility (benefit, advantage, pleasure, or good) by releasing dopamine, a neurotransmitter that creates a sensation of satisfaction, benefit, advantage, pleasure, or good. While these findings explain much about the physiological nature of decision making and how it may directly relate to rational choice theory, they do not explain why my brother loves liver and I do not.

Psychological studies indicate that idiosyncratic utility may have both a cognitive and an affective element. Cognitively, the utility of an object is evaluated on the basis of its essential characteristics. The utility obtained from a particular brand of cigarettes is due to the evaluation of its smell, taste, tar content, price, etc. (Zajonc and Markus 1982, 124). This approach to utility appeals to rational choice theorists because it lends itself well to empirical analysis. The utility of an object is also an affective response, a feeling about the object, that can take place precognitively, post-cognitively, or independent of cognitive evaluation (See Zajonc 1980 and Zajonc and Markus 1982).

Understanding the complex relationship between cognitive and affective elements of utility may help explain the interactions of the individual and social dimensions of utility. Zajonc and Markus (1982) show that affective and cognitive processes interact across both the individual and social dimension of utility in the formation of food preferences. They cite research by Rozin and Schiller (1980) on the acquisition of preferences for chili powder among Mexican children. On a cognitive level, humans are sensitive to the adverse effects of chili powder. Mexican children acquire a taste for chili pepper because their parents introduce it to them in small but increasing amounts beginning around age five. This process is reinforced with social pressures from the family and the community until they want chili pepper in most of the food that they consume. This example calls into question the separability of the individual and social dimensions of utility. How many of our idiosyncratic tastes are created by the social setting?

The social dimension of utility is obtained from the agent's belief and understanding of what is appropriate to desire in the situation of choice. Individuals within social settings are motivated by what they are supposed to do in that setting (March and Olsen 1989, 21). March and Olsen claim that individuals are motivated by the social logic of appropriateness, where "Action involves evoking an identity or role and matching the obligations of that identity or role to a specific situation" (March and Olsen 1998, 951). The agent asks three questions when evaluating courses of action: "What kind of a situation is this? What kind of a person am I? What does a person such as I do in a situation such as this?" (March and Olsen 2004, 4; see also March and Olsen 1989). The logic of consequences represents the individual dimension of utility where actions are evaluated against maximizing the agent's benefits derived from its idiosyncratic tastes. The logic of appropriateness represents the social dimension of utility where actions are evaluated against satisfying the agent's obligations for appropriate behavior in the social setting of choice.

The social dimension of utility is formed as a two-step process under the logic of appropriateness. The agent first evaluates its identity in the social situation of choice and determines what actions are appropriate, given the situation of choice and the agent's identity within it. Utility is then gained from the satisfaction of fulfilling the appropriate actions. The agent's identity in the situation of choice determines the agent's appropriate actions. When the agent asks, "What kind of agent am I?" the agent is not asking about its internal characteristics such as personality, it is asking about what kind of agent it is relative to the social setting (Sending 2002, 449). It is asking about what rules and obligations of the social setting may establish its appropriate actions. Ole Sending emphasizes this point.

By determining an identity, the actor slips into a framework in which the duties and obligations of that identity provide the motivations for appropriate action, the performance of which comes through the application of a rule that specifies what is appropriate in the particular situation (Sending 2002, 449).

Rules determine what actions are appropriate for the situation (March and Olsen 2004, 7). They store "information about institutional practices, routines and norms that tell the actor what to do in a specific situation in order to behave as his or her institutional identity demands" (Sending 2002, 450).

Some constructivist scholars criticize both the logic of consequences and the logic of appropriateness in what they have termed the practice turn in international relations (see Neumann 2002; Pouliot 2008; Hopf 2010, Pouliot and Cornut 2015; and the June 2012 special issue of *Millennium* edited by de Felice and Obino). The logic of consequences is derived from Max Weber's instrumental rationality where "the end, the means, and the secondary results are all rationally taken into account and weighed. This involves rational consideration of alternative means to the end, of the relations of the end to the secondary consequences, and finally of the relative importance of different possible ends" (Weber 1978, 26). The logic of appropriateness is associated with Weber's value-rationality, which is "determined by the conscious belief in the value of its own sake of some ethical, aesthetic, religious, or other form of behavior, independent of its prospects of success" (Weber 1978, 24–25). The logic of practice is based on Weber's traditional rationality that is "determined by ingrained habituation" (Weber 1978, 25). Pouliot (2008, 258) asserts that "what people do, in world politics as in any other social field, does not derive from conscious deliberation or thoughtful reflection—instrumental, rule-based, communicative, or otherwise. Instead, practices are the result of inarticulate, practical knowledge that makes what is to be done appear 'self-evident' or commonsensical." This logic denies utility calculus altogether. Hopf (2010, 541) goes further to define a logic of habit where habits "imply actions by giving us ready-made responses to the world that we execute without thinking." Decisions based on traditional rationality are not intentional behaviors. Traditional rationality, as Weber (1978, 25) points out, "lies very close to the borderline of what can be called meaningfully oriented action, and indeed often on the other side."

The logics of practice and habit provide no theory of motivation. Where utility, norms, and rules provide justification for action in the logics of consequences and appropriateness, action under the logics of practice and habit are derived solely from prior experience. As Hopf (2002, 12) states, "Generally, norms have the form 'in circumstance X, you should do Y,' whereas habits have a general form more like 'in circumstance X, action Y follows.'" As such, the logic of practice and the logic of habit provide little insight into why an agent may or may not contribute to a global public good.

The agent's utility is a synthesis of the individual dimension of utility and the social dimension of utility. Risse (2000) proposes that utility is a continuum with the utility maximizing logic of consequences on one end and the rule-guided logic of appropriateness on the other. He inserts a logic of arguing as a basis for action between these two poles, in which the agent tries to establish whether its assumptions about cause and effect relationships are valid and deliberates with other agents about which norms apply. "Argumentative and deliberative behavior is as goal oriented as strategic interaction, but the goal is not to attain one's fixed preferences, but to seek a reasoned consensus" (Risse 2000, 7).

Many authors equate preferences and utility. This is understandable since utility is mostly unobserved and since the common revealed preference model equates choice and preference without specific reference to utility. Preferences reflect utility but they are not the same as utility. Preferences only emerge in comparison. If I go to my refrigerator for a piece of fruit, and all I find is an apple, I eat the apple and gain utility from it. If my refrigerator contains an apple and an orange, I must address my preference for the fruit by comparing the utility I expect to receive from each and I select the one that I expect will give me the greatest utility.

Preferences are constructed from utility contextually or experientially. If I am buying fruit rather than taking it from my refrigerator, my preference for apples and oranges will likely include other information about the situation of the choice, such as price and the amount of money I have to spend. If the price of an orange is twice as much as the price of an apple, I may prefer to buy the apple even though I get more utility from eating the orange.

Although rational choice theory rejects interpersonal comparisons of utility, it is through comparison that preferences are experientially constructed. Martin Hollis notes that even the simplest preferences that generate supply and demand are constructed through comparison of experiences.

> Indeed, the simplest questions of supply and demand can be discussed "objectively," in terms of people's willingness to pay, only if one can compare the satisfactions which money makes possible. The study of economics could hardly get off the ground without making interpersonal comparisons of utility. (Heap et al. 1992, 328)

Druckman and Lupia contend that the comparisons of utility needed to form preferences are derived from beliefs about the attributes of choices. These beliefs depend on information that results from "interactions between the brain, body, and world" (Druckman and Lupia 2000, 5). Nicholas Onuf suggests that preferences are socially constructed through a complex set of intrapersonal, interpersonal, and global comparisons (Onuf 1989, 265–270).

Preferences result from the synthesis of the individual dimension of utility, evaluated through the logic of consequences, and the social dimension of utility, evaluated through the logic of appropriateness. In this way, preferences are, at least in part, socially constructed.

IDENTITY AND INTERESTS

Identity plays a very important role in forming the social dimension of utility, and therefore, a very important role in the creation of preferences and choice. Peter Berger (1966, 107–108) describes this process in detail. All societies have many different social identities that form part of the objective knowledge of the society. Individual agents internalize these identities as they are socialized into the society. From this internalization, the agent knows who it is. It no longer needs to turn to society to understand its identity. The identity defines the agent's appropriate behavior that becomes the foundation of its social dimension of utility. The agent can conduct itself, "spontaneously, because the firmly internalized cognitive and emotive structures make it unnecessary or even impossible for him (the agent) to reflect upon alternative possibilities of conduct" (Berger 1966, 107). But identities do more than simply define appropriate behavior. They create the psychological reality for the agent. "The individual realizes himself in society—that is, he recognizes his identity in socially defined terms and these definitions become reality as he lives in society." (Berger 1966, 108).

Berger's description of individual identity holds in international relations as well, where agents, such as states, determine their appropriate behaviors from the identities they take on in situations of choice. Even neorealism, that sees states as functionally undifferentiated units, has a theory of identity generating interests. States that identify as "status quo" states are motivated to maintain system order to ensure that the balance of power is not disrupted. States that identify as "revisionist" states seek to acquire as much power as possible by conquest, subjugation, or manipulation (see Waltz 1979; Wendt 1999, 104–105; or Mearsheimer 2013). Waltz explicitly recognizes this connection between the social setting (structure) and utility and behavior through his theory of structural selection.

> The first way in which structures work their effects is through a process of socialization that limits and molds behavior. The second way is through competition . . . Socialization encourages similarities of attributes and of behavior. So does competition. Competition generates an order, the units of which adjust their relations through their autonomous decisions and acts. (Waltz 1979, 76)

In Waltz's neorealism, socialization involves learning the identities embedded in the objective knowledge of international society. Agents, or states, acquire their identities in relation to the structure of the system defined by anarchy and the distribution of capabilities. Through this socialization, the states internalize the actions and desires that are appropriate for the identities they take on. Competition then serves to spur "the actors to accommodate their ways to the socially most acceptable and successful practices," (Waltz 1979, 77) because competition rewards successful behavior with survival and punishes inappropriate behavior with elimination.

Constructivist theory of international relations takes a much broader view of the role of identities and interests. Wendt (1999, 224) treats identity as "a property of intentional actors that generates motivational and behavioral dispositions." He claims that "Interests presuppose identities because an actor cannot know what it wants until it knows who it is." (Wendt 1999, 231). Ole Sending captures the relationship between an agent's socially defined identity and its utility elegantly:

> The underlying idea here is that the self becomes social through acquiring and fulfilling institutional identities. An institutionally defined identity thus demands certain actions in order for that identity to be fulfilled and maintained. When actors act according to appropriate rules, they do not do so because there are external sanctions that compel them to do so, nor is it some perception of self-interest. Rather, it is because the individual actor has internalized the duties and obligations that define an institutional identity that the actor acts as he or she does. (Sending 2002, 449)

ACCOUNTING FOR TASTES—MODELING AND INTERPRETING THE EFFECTS OF UTILITIES

Rational choice theory is informed by a scientific realist epistemology even though most analysts do not realize, recognize, or admit this. Although there are many different approaches to scientific realism, its three basic tenets are the following. First, the world exists as real things—real physical objects, real effects of relationships, and real understandings, beliefs, and perceptions. The objects of science are the structures and mechanisms that generate phenomena. The objects "are neither phenomena . . . nor human constructs imposed upon phenomena . . . but real structures which endure and operate independently of our knowledge, experience, or the conditions that allow us to access them" (Bhaskar 1975, 25). Simply because these structures may exist in our mind does not mean that they are not real. This is a critical point when scientific realism is applied to rational choice. The reality of the choice situation is defined by the understandings of the chooser—its perception of the material constraints, the likelihood of success, and its own utility calculation.

Second, to understand the world is to understand the relationships between real phenomena and the real characteristics of the world that cause the phenomena (causal factors). Scientific realism is a causal theory. The world exists as a set of real causal relationships that link real causal factors with real phenomena. The real phenomena may be phenomena of the physical world or of the mind and the real causal factors may be observable or unobservable. The epistemology of scientific realism requires that the relationship between phenomenon and cause be a real causal relationship.

Finally, causal factors include observed characteristics of the world as well as unobserved characteristics of the world. Scientific realists accept an unobserved entity's existence if it can "produce observable effects, or if its manipulation permits us to intervene with effect in the observable world" (Wendt 1987, 352). Jackson, following Bhaskar, calls this quality of scientific realism "transfactualism" and refers to it as "the possibility of going beyond the facts to grasp the deeper processes and factors that generate those facts" (Jackson 2011, 37; see also Wight 2006, 18 and Bhaskar 1975, 14). Weldes (1989, 367) claims that this is a fundamental difference with empiricism in terms of justifying ontological claims. Where empiricists justify the existence of a claim based on observability, scientific realists accept the existence of unobservable phenomena that may have observable effects.

Since causal factors that affect real phenomena may transcend observation, their effect must be interpreted rather than observed. One way to do this is to create a model that represents the causal relationships between real phenomena and the observed and unobserved causal factors and then determine the effects on the phenomena when the observation of the observed causal factors and the interpretation of the unobserved causal factors vary. This type of model is a representation of theoretical, not empirical, relationships.

Clarke and Primo believe that models in political science should be thought of as maps. Maps may only be lines drawn on a page. They are not isomorphic with the reality they depict in any significant way. A map is neither true nor false. Its value lies only in the degree to which it represents some aspect of reality in a useful way. Clarke and Primo state that

> political scientists should think of models more like representational objects and less like linguistic entities. That is, we argue that models in political science should be viewed as maps rather than statements, and we should be asking of our models whether they are similar enough to the world *to be used for specific purposes*. (Clarke and Primo 2007, 742; emphasis in the original)

This quotation raises two important issues about models. First, although they may contain linguistic content, models are representations that come in many forms. Second, models are constructed for specific uses and purposes. They do not need to be representations of the whole world. Models represent some portion of reality for some particular use. The iconic pirate's map may be no more than a sketch of dotted lines indicating that one should start at a particular palm tree and take ten paces north then five paces west, and "X marks the spot!" A model of a molecule in chemistry may be a set of lines on a page that represents valence bonds between atoms. A model in micro-economics may be a graph representing observable quantities and unobservable utilities. A model should be evaluated on the basis of whether or not it is a sufficient representation of reality to meet the purpose for which it was intended. The usefulness of these models turns on their suitability for representing the systems that are their subjects. "A model, then, may or may not be suitable; it always has its limitations; but it is not either true or false, or subject to what is usually called induction" (Hutten 1954, 296). Testing a model "becomes a matter not of 'confirming a prediction,' but assessing whether the degree of similarity between two systems is sufficient for a specific purpose" (Clarke and Primo 2007, 247), or as Patrick Jackson states, it "is more about calibrating the model than about falsifying it" (Jackson 2011, 147).

I develop a model in chapter 3 that represents the situation of choice for an individual agent deciding whether or not to contribute to a public good. The model is presented in graphic form. It includes representations of observable characteristics of the situation of choice such as the price of the public good, the endowment of resources of the individual, and the perceived amount of public good that the agent expects the rest of the collective to provide. The model also includes representations of unobservable characteristics of the situation of choice such as the utility that the individual agents receives from various amounts of the public good. The structure of the model should be familiar to any student of micro-economics.

The purpose of the model is to illustrate how various levels of the observed characteristics of the situation of choice (price, endowment, etc.) interact with different levels of unobserved characteristics (utility) that are interpreted from the agent's culture, history, and internal and external political situation that establish its identity in the situation of choice. The model is a rational choice model in every sense. It is based on the rationality principle as expressed in preferences that adhere to the standard rationality postulates. However, the driving force for choice in the model is the interpretation of the unobserved utilities that determine the agent's preferences for different outcomes of a public goods decision. Those utility-driven preferences are then compared to the collective using simple games to explain outcomes in public goods decisions in the areas of leadership of the global economy, protecting human rights, and providing collective security. Although I may criticize rational choice theory, it is not my intention to reject it. The goal of this book is to illustrate that rational choice models become much more robust representations of reality when theorists engage in thick rationality (Ferejohn 1991) and develop understandings of the deep unobserved causal factors that affect choice.

Interpreting how utilities affect choice is a three-step process. First, the identity of the agent relative to the other agents in the situation of choice must be established. Then the interests (utilities) generated by that identity must be cataloged. Finally, the effect of the utilities on preferences and choice must be derived. The last of these three steps is achieved by the models developed in the next chapter. The first two steps, however, means a rational choice explanation of the decision to provide public good must begin with interpretive research.

The concept of identity is complex. Many approaches and definitions abound. Erik Erickson (1950 and 1968) introduced identity in developmental psychology in the 1950s and 1960s. The social sciences embraced identity in the 1970s and 1980s with role identity theory in sociology and social identity theory in psychology. Identity became a major conceptual variable in international relations with the emergence of constructivist approaches in the 1990s.[2] I define identity as a combination of the role that an agent plays in its interactions with other agents and the package of rules that is needed to establish and maintain that role. It is this package of rules that connects the identity with interests and utilities. Nicholas Onuf claimed that "Rules describe some class of actions and indicate whether these actions constitute warranted conduct on the part of those to whom these rules are addressed" (Onuf 1994, 10). I have defined rules elsewhere as "statements that define classes of actions from which rational actors draw inferences about which class of actions may lead to higher utility and thereby be performed (Roberts 1997, 165). In both of these definitions, rules are statements about what actions are appropriate for an agent to satisfy its interests or gain utility.

To discover an identity is to discover its role vis-á-vis others and the rules that sustain the identity. Roles are discovered through interpretive history and genealogy. Rules are discovered through linguistic analysis of documents, statements, and actions. In the following chapters, these methods will be used to interpret the unobserved identities and utilities of agents engaged in choosing whether or not to participate in the provision of public goods. The effect of identities and utilities will be illustrated (not predicted!) through the models developed in chapter 3.

NOTES

1. Stigler (1950a, 1950b) traced utility theory in economics from its roots in the work of Smith and Bentham to its abandonment in the mid-twentieth century.

2. See Brubaker and Cooper (2000) for a general discussion of the many approaches to identity. See Hogg et al. (1995) for an overview of identity theory in psychology and sociology. See Lebow (2008) for a discussion of identity and international relations.

THREE

Utility, Preferences, and the
Individual Public Goods Decision

CURRENT MODELS OF THE PUBLIC GOODS DECISION

Individuals decide whether or not to provide public goods. They do so as part of a group, but the decision is always an individual decision. Since Mancur Olson published *The Logic of Collective Action* in 1965, much of the literature on public goods focused on the characteristics of groups and the interactions that occur within those groups. Who are the individuals that constitute these groups? Why do individual agents participate in the provision of a public good? While Olson centered his argument on groups, he did not lose sight of the importance of the individual's motivation to provide the good within the group. Privileged groups have at least some members who benefit enough from the provision of the public goods that they are willing to provide the good even if no one else is willing to provide the good. Intermediate groups have members who receive enough benefit from the good to want it provided, but they have no incentive to be the sole provider. However, in small intermediate groups, interaction between the members might bring about provision of the good. Latent group members benefit from the good, but their benefit is so small relative to the cost that there is no incentive within the context of the good itself that makes them want to provide the good. Latent groups tend to be so large that strategic interaction has no effect because the action of any individual group member is effectively invisible to the rest of the members. Latent group members could be encouraged to supply the good if a large enough selective incentive is offered as a reward or if free riders receive a significant punishment.

Analysts often propose simple game models of public goods because they replicate observed public goods behavior. As Russell Hardin (1982, 25) stated, "Indeed the problem of collective action and the Prisoners' Dilemma are essentially the same." Choosing a game model because it replicates an observed outcome, however, is tautological. Such a model merely mimics the phenomenon in question. It does not add to our store of knowledge.

I take a different approach. In chapter 2, I argued that an agent's identity determines, in part, the agent's desires, wants, and interests—that is, its utilities. Preferences for different outcomes, then, are derived from the agent's utilities and the social and material constraints that are part of the situation of choice. These constraints include the cost of different options, the preferences of the other agents involved in the choice, and the agent's endowment of resources. As a rational choice model, choice is determined by the agent's utilities and preferences.

The goal of this chapter is to develop a utility-based model of the individual's decision to contribute to the provision of a public good. I develop the model in two stages. I begin by determining the preference orderings that an agent can logically have for the outcomes of simple public goods games played between the individual and the rest of the collective. Then I develop a model that shows how these possible preferences are derived from the agent's utilities and the situation of choice. The model does not indicate how utilities are socially constructed from the agent's identity. That task is an interpretive task that will be illustrated in case studies in subsequent chapters. While the work presented here has significant implications for optimum outcomes for the collective, it only addresses the individual's decision, not the Pareto efficiency of the outcome for the society or group.

Scholarship on the provision of public goods can roughly be classified into three categories that parallel Olson's three criteria above.[1] The first category of scholarship provides explanations of why individuals contribute to the provision of public goods based on the utility calculus of various outcomes of public goods interactions. Two general conclusions are drawn from this literature. First, the individual will only contribute to the provision of a public good if the utility gained from providing additional supply of the public good exceeds the individual's costs. Second, utility maximizing behavior among individuals may result in a Nash equilibrium for the collective, but that equilibrium may not be Pareto optimal (see for example: Buchanan 1968; Cornes and Sandler 1996; Fogarty 1981; Mueller 1989; Sandler 1992; and Sugden 1982). The literature also includes alternative approaches that try to resolve this public goods dilemma by incorporating non-pecuniary values, such as altruism or inequality-aversion, into the individual's utility schedule (Ahn et al. 2003; Andreoni 1988, 1990, and 1995; Makris 2009; and Sugden 1982). These authors propose that the public good may be provided in a group with heterogeneous preferences by individuals who forego individual benefit for the benefit of the collective. As Sugden (1982, 349) states, "if one interprets 'utility' in the classical Benthamite way, as a psychological experience of pleasure, it is not a matter of logical necessity that an individual should seek to maximize his own utility." Ahn et al. (2003) operationalize this "Benthamite" approach by proposing a public goods game with the pecuniary values that represent the outcomes of a Prisoner's Dilemma but then show that preferences for altruism and inequality-aversion over those outcomes can result in preference orderings other than the all-defect equilibrium of the Prisoner's Dilemma game. Fehr and Schmidt (1999) show that equity considerations affect public goods outcomes even in large, highly competitive groups. Other variables that affect the individual's utility calculus in public goods decisions include the relative scale of the payoffs (Ahn et al. 2001), the initial endowments of the individuals (Bergstrom et al., 1986), and information about other actors' intentions (Austen-Smith 1980).

The second body of public goods literature explores the effect of group size on the provision of a public good (see Frohlich and Oppenheimer 1970; Hardin 1971; Pecorino 1999; Esteban and Ray 2001; Pecorino and Temimi 2007 and 2008). Olson identified three factors that keep large groups from providing the collective good. First, the larger the group, the smaller the benefit any one agent will receive as a reward for providing the good. Second, with smaller rewards, subsets of members trying to provide the good will not be able to afford the cost. Finally, larger groups require higher organization costs for rallying members to provide the good (Olson 1971, 48).

The literature on group size disputes Olson's claims from a number of perspectives. Hardin (1971) showed that if the public goods decision is characterized as a n-person Prisoner's Dilemma where the players chose from the 2^n different outcomes of the interaction rather than simply choosing to contribute or not to the public good, there are Condorcet outcomes that are individually and Pareto superior to the normally dominant all-defect strategy. Frohlich and Oppenheimer (1970) demonstrated that the decision to free-ride is a function of the individual's ability to estimate the likely donations of others to determine the efficacy of its own contribution to the provision of the public good. They concluded that "given that the free-rider effects need not be a function of changing group-size, the extent of the free-rider problem, in groups of any size, will depend on the existence of a coordinating mechanism. Without such a mechanism there is no a priori reason to believe that goods will be collectively supplied to groups of any size" (Frohlich and Oppenheimer 1970, 119).

Group size is also examined in the context of the dynamics of n-person games. Nunn and Watkins found the existence of non-cooperative mixed strategy equilibria in n-person public goods games where the players had the same expected utility if they did not contribute, always contributed, or randomly contributed with the same probability as all others. This led them to conclude that "there can be a voluntary, although imperfect, resolution of the public goods problem" (Nunn and Watkins 1978, 606).

Other authors found that the dynamics of the n-person game can create coalitions of contributors that then grow into grand coalitions (Schofield 1977) and that by applying optimal auctions to the public goods decision, the importance of the free-rider problem diminishes as the size of the group increases (Bliss and Nalebuff 1984).

The third body of literature examines the effect of the structure of the public goods interaction and the protocols of the games that are used to model the public goods decision. Four major variables addressed in this literature are incentives, aggregation technologies, iterated interactions, and the preference orderings that are used in public goods games. One approach is to model selective incentive and punishments as side payments in the utility calculus for providing public goods (see Aggarwal and Dupont 1999, 2002, and 2003; Holzinger 2003; Wallner 2002; Fehr and Schmidt 2005; and Fowler and Harpending 2005). Medina (2005, 427) proposes a stochastic public goods model from which he claims that as the number of participants increases, "the benefits of cooperation are irrelevant for explaining collective action. In deciding whether to cooperate, individuals *only* consider the value of the selective incentive and the cost of cooperation" (emphasis in the original).

Some literature on the protocols of public goods models explores aggregation technologies—the process by which contributions are accumulated and spent to provide a public good (Sandler 2015, 198). Three aggregation technologies are generally discussed: lumpy goods (also known as threshold goods); best-shot goods; and weakest-link goods. Lumpy or threshold goods can only be produced if a certain threshold of contributions can be amassed. For example, voluntary contributions to complete a community bridge over a ravine only return a benefit if enough resources are accumulated to complete the bridge. Half a bridge benefits no one. Contributors to lumpy goods face the possibility that their contributions will be lost if the threshold is not met.

The total quantity of a best-shot good is determined only by the maximum individual contribution. Lesser contributors to a best-shot good are wasting their money. The total supply of weakest-link goods depends only on the smallest individual contribution. Other agents who try to increase the supply of weakest-link goods are also wasting their money. Hirshleifer (1983) shows that weakest-link goods are less likely to be under supplied while best-shot goods are more likely to be under supplied. Sandler (1992 and 1998) derives two-person game models that represent best-shot and weakest-link goods and uses these models to show that a more equal distribution of income is likely to increase the supply of weakest-link goods while a top-heavier income distribution is likely to increase the supply of best-shot goods.

Another aspect of the public goods protocol is the effect of iterated play. Even the intransigent all-defect strategy of the Prisoner's Dilemma is dominated by Pareto optimal cooperative strategies in extended play with a sufficiently high future discounting factor. Authors explore the effect of extended play on free-riding (Fershtman and Nitzan 1991); they demonstrate how different strategies, such as tit-for-tat, can generate socially efficient outcomes in iterated games (Axelrod 1980, 1981, and 1984; Lichbach 1992); and they compare the performance of different games, such as Prisoner's Dilemma and Assurance, in modeling public goods provision in repeated play (Runge 1984). Hechter (1992), however, raises the specter of the Folk Theorem as a warning against relying too heavily on the multiple equilibria that can emerge in infinitely repeated games.

Finally, there is a substantial literature that proposes different game structures as the preferred public goods model. The Prisoner's Dilemma game is used as a public goods model in a host of literature (see, for example: Ahn et al. 2003; Archetti and Scheuring 2012; Austen-Smith 1980; Fogarty 1981; Hardin 1971; Hirshleifer 1999; Holzinger 2003; Kollock 1998; Medina 2005; Taylor 1987; and Wallner 2002). Other authors (see DeCanio, and Fremstad 2013; Heckathorn 1996; Kollock 1998; and Lipnowski and Maital 1983) derive the preference conditions needed for the game of Chicken to represent the public goods decisions. A number of authors propose the Assurance game as an alternative game (see: Ahn et al. 2003; Frohlich et al. 1975; Runge 1984; and Taylor 1987).

Evolutionary games have recently been used to examine how cooperative strategies such as the Assurance game invade populations of players engaged in conflictive games such as the Prisoner's Dilemma (see Archetti and Scheuring 2012; Santos et al. 2008; Perc and Szolnoki 2010; and Wang et al. 2010). Heckathorn (1996), Kollock (1998), Sandler (2004 and 2015); and Taylor (1987) provide thorough discussions of different types of public goods games and when to use them.

What is lacking in these discussions of different public goods games, and in the public goods literature in general, is a thorough examination of the *individual's* decision whether or not to contribute to the public good. The individual is often overlooked because, except in very small groups, the success or failure of the public goods problem is determined by the choices of the group as a whole, not by an individual. There are exceptions to this, such as international relations, where a few very powerful agents can significantly affect the population's supply of the good. Even in the largest, most impersonal group, the choice to provide or not provide the good is ultimately made by the individual agent, based on its own preferences for the outcomes of a public goods interaction. The structure and formation of these preferences, therefore, should be the starting place for theories of public goods.

THE INDIVIDUAL'S DECISION TO CONTRIBUTE
TO A PUBLIC GOOD

The decision whether or not to contribute voluntarily toward the provision of a public good can be characterized as a decision to exchange a private good numeraire (such as money) for some quantity of a public good.[2] Since the good is public, any quantity that the individual purchases with the numeraire will be available to all members of the collective. When contributing toward the provision of the public good, the individual will likely take into consideration the amount of good that it expects the rest of the collective to provide. For definition, let X be a quantity of the public good, let Y be a quantity of the private good numeraire, and let y be the individual's initial endowment of private good numeraire. Let the private good numeraire be defined in such a way that there is a 1 to 1 price ratio of private good to public good. Thus, if the individual spends α units of private good it will supply α units of public good to the collective.[3] Let β represent the quantity of the public good that the individual expects to be provided by the rest of the collective as a whole.[4] Let U_x and U_y represent the utilities obtained from increments of public good X and private good Y, respectively, ceteris paribus.

The individual's decision can be modeled in the matrix shown in figure 3.1. If neither the individual nor the collective provides any public good, the individual's utility is derived solely from its endowment of private good [$U_y(y)$]. If the individual *alone* pays α units of its endowment of private good toward the provision of the public good, it benefits from the α units of public good it provides to the collective but its utility from the private good numeraire is reduced by the amount it pays for the public good. The individual's net utility of this transaction is $U_x(\alpha)+U_y(y-\alpha)$. If the individual free-rides, it retains the utility from its entire endowment of private good and it gains the utility from the amount of public good provided by the rest of the collective [$U_x(\beta)+U_y(y)$]. If the individual collectively contributes to the provision of the public good, its utility is the sum of the stock of public good produced by it and the collective plus the utility from its remaining endowment of the private good numeraire after it pays for the public good [$U_x(\alpha+\beta)+U_y(y-\alpha)$]. Each cell in figure 3.1 denotes the net utility of the decision outcome.

The individual does not see the other players individually. The individual's utility of the collective's supply of the good is $U_x(\beta)$ and the individual sees the utility of its own supply of the good as $U_x(\alpha)$, which may, or may not, equal any other individual's supply of the good. Thus, if the individual participates in the collective provision of the good, it adds its

	Collective:	
Individual:	Do Not Contribute (D)	Contribute (C)
Do Not Contribute (D)	DD = $U_y(y)$	DC = $U_x(\beta)+U_y(y)$
Contribute (C)	CD = $U_x(\alpha)+U_y(y-\alpha)$	CC = $U_x(\alpha+\beta)+U_y(y-\alpha)$

Figure 3.1.   The individual's public goods decision matrix. *Source*: author.

quantity to the collective quantity and this sum is then available to all the members of the group $(\alpha+\beta)$. If the individual free-rides, it merely enjoys the collective supply of the public good along with the rest of the collective.

The model described above embodies a number of assumptions about the behavior of the individual and about the individual's valuation of the private and public goods. First, both the private and public goods are goods, that is, $U_x(X) > 0$ and $U_y(Y) > 0$ for all values of X and Y greater than zero. Since the model represents the interactive decision of an individual, it is assumed that the individual expects that some level of public good may be provided by the rest of the collective. This means that $\beta > 0$ and thus $U_x(\beta) > 0$. Although most of the following argument will treat utilities as cardinal values, there is nothing in the argument that requires that utilities have more than ordinal value. Utilities are assumed to be additive and distributive. That is, $U_x(X+X') = U_x(X)+U_x(X')$ and $U_y(Y+Y') = U_y(Y)+U_y(Y')$ for all X, X', Y, and Y'. One more restriction is placed upon the model to make its specification easier. The marginal rate of substitution in consumption (MRSc) is assumed to be constant for all values of X at the endowment value of y. That is, the marginal utility of cell DD is the same as the marginal utility of cell DC in figure 3.1.[5] This may be reasonable if the decision by the individual in figure 3.1 is made without knowledge of the action taken by the rest of the collective or if the decisions of both players are made simultaneously. Nonetheless, this restriction will be relaxed later.

Given these assumptions and the definitions of the individual utility values for each possible outcome of the game in figure 3.1 (DD, DC, CD, CC), the possible preference orderings for an individual can be derived through a set of simple algebraic proofs that are shown in the appendix to chapter 3.

POSSIBLE PREFERENCE ORDERINGS
IN THE 2 X 2 PUBLIC GOODS GAME

The 4! possible ordinal preference orderings for the 2 x 2 variable sum game are shown in table 3.1. All but four of these preference orderings can be eliminated from consideration due to the requirements of theorems 1, 6, and 7 or corollary 7.1 discussed in the appendix to chapter 3. That is, no permutation in which CD > CC, DD > DC, (DC > CC and CD > DD), or (CC > DD and DD > CD) can be a preference ordering, given the assumptions of the model at this point and the arguments in the previous discussion.

Figure 3.2 depicts a utility-based model of an agent's decision to contribute to the provision of a public good in graphic form.[6] The model shows the relationship between the individual's utilities and the situation of choice that includes the amount of the public good the individual expects that the rest of the collective will provide, the constraining effect of the individual's endowment of private good numeraire, and the market rate of exchange between the private numeraire and the public good. The individual's utilities are shown as indifference curves. Each curve represents combinations of the public good and the private good numeraire that provide equal overall utility for the individual. That is, the total utility of the agent does not change as the individual trades numeraire for public good along any given indifference curve. The individual's total

Table 3.1.   The 24 permutations of the public goods preference orderings.

Permutation	Possible?	Reason not Possible	Permutation	Possible?	Reason not Poss
1. **CC > CD > DC > DD**	Yes		13. DC > CC > CD > DD	No	Theore
2. CC > CD > DD > DC	No	Theorem 6	14. **DC > CC > DD > CD**	Yes	
3. **CC > DC > CD > DD**	Yes		15. DC > CD > CC > DD	No	Theore
4. CC > DC > DD > CD	No	Corollary 7.1	16. DC > CD > CC > DD	No	Theore
5. CC > DD > CD > DC	No	Theorem 6	17. **DC > DD > CC > CD**	Yes	
6. CC > DD > DC > CD	No	Theorem 6	18. DC > DD > CD > CC	No	Theore
7. CD > CC > DC > DD	No	Theorem 1	19. DD > CC > CD > DC	No	Theore
8. CD > CC > DD > DC	No	Theorem 1	20. DD > CC > DC > CD	No	Theore
9. CD > DC > CC > DD	No	Theorem 1	21. DD > CD > CC > DC	No	Theore
10. CD > DC > DD > CC	No	Theorem 1	22. DD > CD > DC > CC	No	Theore
11. CD > DD > CC > DC	No	Theorem 1	23. DD > DC > CC > CD	No	Theore
12. CD > DD > DC > CC	No	Theorem 1	24. DD > DC > CD > CC	No	Theore

Private Good (Y)

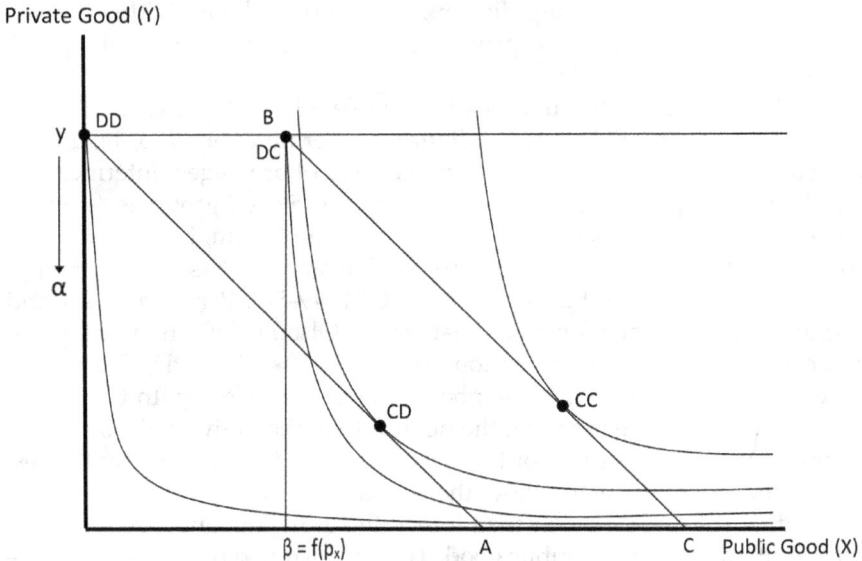

Figure 3.2. The special privileged utility model (CC > CD > DC > DD). *Source*: author.

utility is higher on indifference curves further away from the origin of the graph.[7] The marginal rate of substitution in consumption (MRSc) is the slope of any indifference curve at some point. The MRSc represents the rate at which the private numeraire can be traded for public good or the public good can be traded for the numeraire at that point on the curve without affecting the agent's overall utility.

The quantity of public good (X) is represented by the horizonal axis while the quantity of private good numeraire (Y) is represented by the vertical axis. The individual is assumed to have an initial endowment of y units of private good that can be paid to obtain units of the public good. The fixed 1:1 exchange rate, illustrated by lines $\overline{yA}$, and $\overline{BC}$ represent the exchange value of the good in terms of the private good. Points along $\overline{yA}$ represent the CD outcome of the previous discussion, since they represent the individual's provision of the good without assistance from the collective. Points along the horizontal line at y represent free-riding where various levels of public good are provided by the collective alone while the individual maintains its endowment of y units of private good. The individual expects the public good supplied by the collective to be β. Thus, the point DC represents the individual's perception of the supply of public and private goods when free-riding. Points along line $\overline{yA}$ represent the joint provision outcome (CC) when both the individual and the collective provide some quantity of the public good. If neither the individual nor the collective supplies the public good, the individual retains its initial endowment (y) of private good and receives no public good, representing outcome DD.

The four possible permutations from table 3.1 can be illustrated using the utility-based model shown in figure 3.2. Permutations 1, 3, 14, and 17 directly correspond to Mancur Olson's concept of privileged, intermediate, and latent group members. Olson defined a privileged group as "a group such that each of its members, or at least some of them, has an incentive to see that the collective good is provided, even if he has to bear the full burden of providing it himself" (Olson 1971, 49–50). Permutations 1 and 3 represent preference functions that satisfy Olson's definition of a privileged group member. Permutation 1 (CC > CD > DC > DD) is a special case of the privileged group member's preference ordering. In the special privileged preference function, the net utility of the individual's own contribution exceeds the value of the good that may be provided by the rest of the collective. In such a case, the individual prefers sole provision to free-riding (CD > DC) rather than forego the utility obtained from its own contribution toward the public good. This is illustrated on figure 3.2 where the steepness of the marginal rate of substitution in consumption (the slope of the indifference curves), at point DC ensures that there is a point (CD) along the budget line that provides greater utility than the point DC.[8]

An electric power company that provides resources for energy conservation activities within its service area is a good example of an actor with the special privileged preference ordering. The power company is able to provide a significant supply of public goods for conservation (special deals on energy saving light bulbs or public service messages) which, while benefitting all consumers in the region, allows the company to divert service from lower rate residential customers to higher rate commercial customers. David Lake (1988, 46) used this special privileged preference ordering to represent the interests of a hegemonic leader in the world economy. A large, economically powerful nation may be willing to provide the public good of stabilizing the world economy by itself rather than face the possibility that no other nation may rise to the task. It would do so if the net benefit it gains from its own stabilization policies exceed the benefit that it expects to obtain from whatever level of stabilization the rest of the nations might provide. This is the heart of "hegemonic stability theory" in the international political economy literature.[9]

Permutation 3 (CC > DC > CD > DD) is a more general case of the privileged group preference.[10] In this case, the individual prefers free-riding to sole provision (DC > CD) but prefers sole provision over no good being provided (CD > DD) because the utility of its own supply of the public good exceeds its costs. Since the benefit of its own supply exceeds its cost, it would willingly participate in the collective provision of the good rather than forego the utility that its own supply will generate. In figure 3.3, the MRSc at point DC is steep enough to ensure that there is some point along $\overline{BC}$ (the joint provision outcome) that will provide higher utility than the free-riding outcome (DC). The MRSc is not so steep that the indifference curve containing the point DC intersects the line. This ensures that free-riding (DC) has a higher utility than sole provision (CD).

Olson's intermediate group is a group "in which no single member gets a share of the benefit sufficient to give him an incentive to provide the good himself, but which does not have so many members that no one member will notice whether any other member is or is not helping to provide the collective good" (Olson 1971, 50). Olson emphasizes that such groups do not normally provide a public good based on utility calculation alone. Due to their small size, however, it is possible for an intermediate group to provide a public good through the dynamics of strategic interaction. As Taylor (1987, 10–11) pointed out, the intermediate group should not be distinguished on size alone, but must be based on the utility of the supply that an individual is able to provide. Indeed, even if the size of the group is small, public goods may not be provided unless the preference orderings of the individual members are susceptible to the dynamics of strategic interaction.

Permutation 14 (DC > CC > DD > CD), which is the preference ordering for the familiar Prisoner's Dilemma game, offers such a susceptible pref-

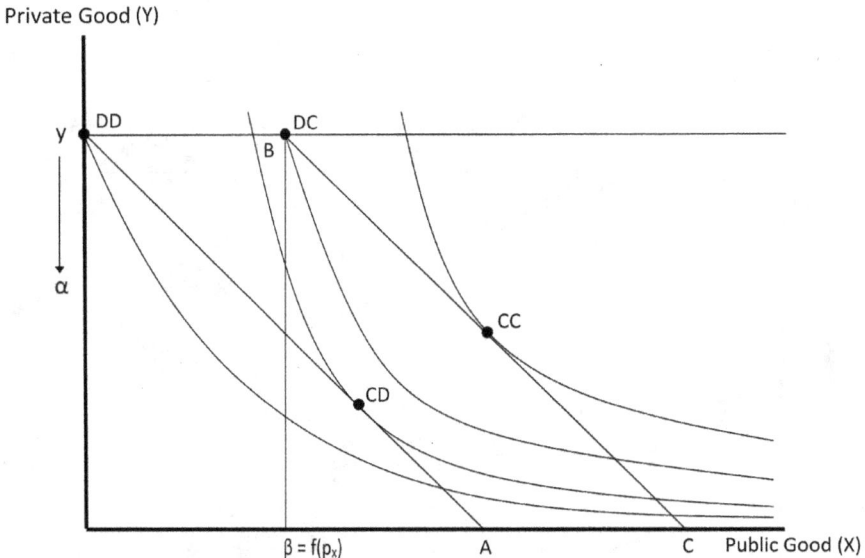

Figure 3.3.   The privileged utility model (CC > DC > CD > DD). *Source*: author.

erence ordering. When $U_y(\alpha+\beta) > U_y(\alpha) > U_x(\alpha)$, the costs of contributing to the good exceed the benefit the individual receives if it is the only contributor $[U_y(\alpha) > U_x(\alpha)]$, but the benefit of collective provision of the good exceeds the costs of the individual's participation $[U_y(\alpha+\beta) > U_y(\alpha)]$. In this case, the individual prefers the benefit of collective provision of the good but is unwilling to risk being the only one contributing to its costs. In figure 3.4, the MRSc at outcome DC is less than 1 guaranteeing a corner solution at point B (see the appendix to chapter 3), meaning that there is no point along $\overline{BC}$ (the joint provision outcome) that has higher utility than free-riding (DC). If the MRSc at outcome DD is also less than 1, which is true by restriction, then no point in the CD outcome set (line $\overline{yA}$) has higher utility than outcome DD. Countless articles and books have discussed the unique qualities of the Prisoner's Dilemma. Many authors have shown that some level of supply of the public good is a likely (or at least possible) outcome of N-player, repeated play, or negotiated models of Prisoner's Dilemma (See, for example, Axelrod 1980, 1981, and 1984; Hardin 1971; Lichbach 1992; and Taylor 1976).

The large latent group in Olson's analysis is least likely to be successful at providing a public good. The group is composed of individuals which "by definition, cannot make a noticeable contribution to any group effort, and since no one in the group will react if he makes no contribution; he has no incentive to contribute" (Olson 1971, 50). Olson contends that such

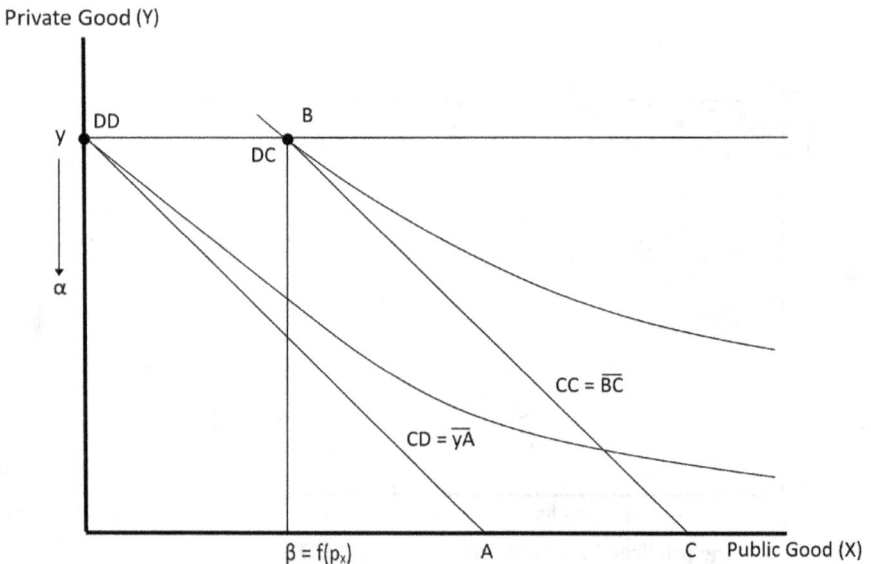

Figure 3.4.   The intermediate utility model (DC > CC > DD > CD). *Source*: author.

latent groups are large relative to their possible contribution to the supply of the good. Individuals in the group must also have preference orderings for the good that are unlikely to be affected by strategic interaction. Permutation 17 (DC > DD > CC > CD) represents the essential qualities of the latent group member's preference ordering. Like the intermediate utility model, DC > CC implies that the individual's costs of providing the good exceed the benefits derived from its own supply. Unlike the intermediate preference ordering, DD > CC implies that costs also exceed the utility of the good supplied by collective provision (see Corollary 3.1 in the appendix to chapter 3). Thus, the latent individual prefers no good being provided to either sole provision or collective provision of the public good. Figure 3.5 illustrates the flat indifference curves that are necessary to obtain this preference ordering in the utility-based model.

The utility-based models of the individual's decision to provide a public good shown in figures 3.2 through 3.5 derive the individual's preferences by illustrating the relationship between the observed situation of choice (endowment, price ratio, and perceived collective contribution) and the unobserved utilities of the individual obtained from quantities of the public and private goods. The individual's optimum allocation between the public and private good and the necessary and sufficient conditions for each preference ordering are derived in the appendix to chapter 3. The unknown causal factor in each graphic model is the structure of the

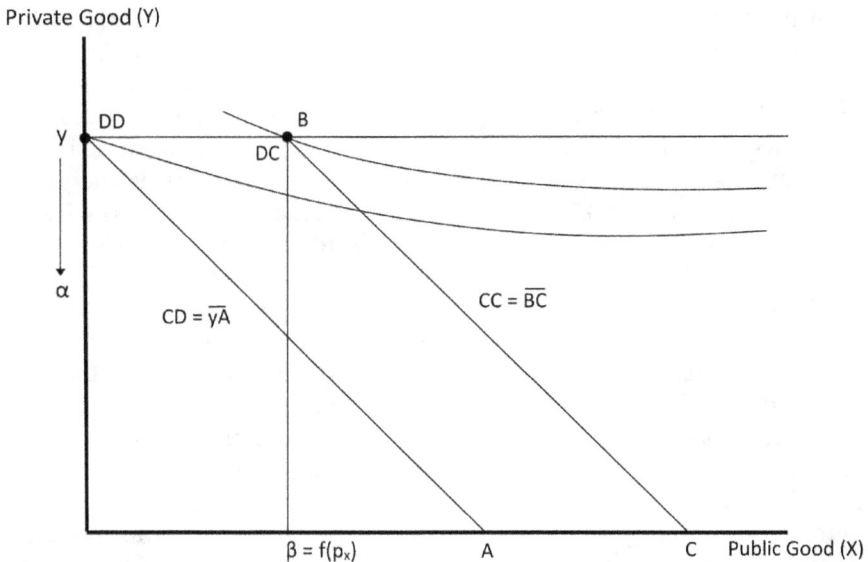

Figure 3.5.   The latent utility model (DC > DD > CC > CD). *Source*: author.

individual's utilities. In these simplified models, that structure is reduced to the relative values the individual places on the public good and the private good numeraire. As I discussed in chapter 2, these utilities are, in part, socially constructed and must be interpreted from the individual's identity in the situation of choice rather than directly observed.

ASSURANCE AND CHICKEN

When the restriction that the marginal rate of substitution in consumption (MRSc) is assumed to be constant for all values of X at the endowment value of y is removed, the logic of Theorem 7 and Corollary 7.1 fails because $U_x(\alpha)$ and $U_y(\alpha)$ need not be constant. Thus, the utility derived from α units of public good may be greater than the utility derived from α units of the numeraire at DD but be less than the utility derived from α units of numeraire at DC. Such would be the case if the individual expected the quantity of public good provided by the rest of the collective (β) to be large enough to sate much of its desire for the public good. When the restriction on MRSc is removed, two other permutations of preference orderings become possible. Permutation 4 (CC > DC > DD > CD), which is the preference ordering for the Assurance or Stag Hunt game, can be a preference ordering when MRSc at outcome DD is less than 1 and the MRSc at outcome DC is greater than 1. This requires increasing marginal returns to utility for increasing levels of X. Variations on the Assurance game have been used to represent more cooperative public goods situations where the group members incorporate preferences for altruism and inequity-aversion (Runge 1984; Ahn et al. 2003) and where group members need to coordinate their contributions in order to provide the public good. Figure 3.6 shows the utility-based model of the Assurance preference function.

Another game used to model the public goods decision is the game of Chicken. Taylor (1987, 35–36) describes a scenario where two willing, privileged players may succumb to the brinkmanship of the game of Chicken as each player waits to see who provides the good first. Sandler (1992, 40–41) says that Chicken could be used to model public goods situations such as averting national disasters or providing needed infrastructure. A variety of authors propose public goods scenarios that are modeled with the game of Chicken. (See, for example: Frohlich et al. 1975; Heckathorn 1996; Hirshleifer 1999; Kollock 1998; Lipnowski and Maital 1983; and Taylor and Ward 1982) The game has no dominant strategies but it has two Pareto optimal Nash equilibria (CD and DC), each obtained by one player acting while the other does not. The worst outcome (DD) occurs when neither player acts as they both wait for the other to act. Permutation 13 (DC > CC > CD > DD) for the game of Chicken can be modeled on the indifference graph if the MRSc at outcome DD is greater than 1 and the MRSc at outcome DC is less than 1. This is shown in figure 3.7.

Private Good (Y)

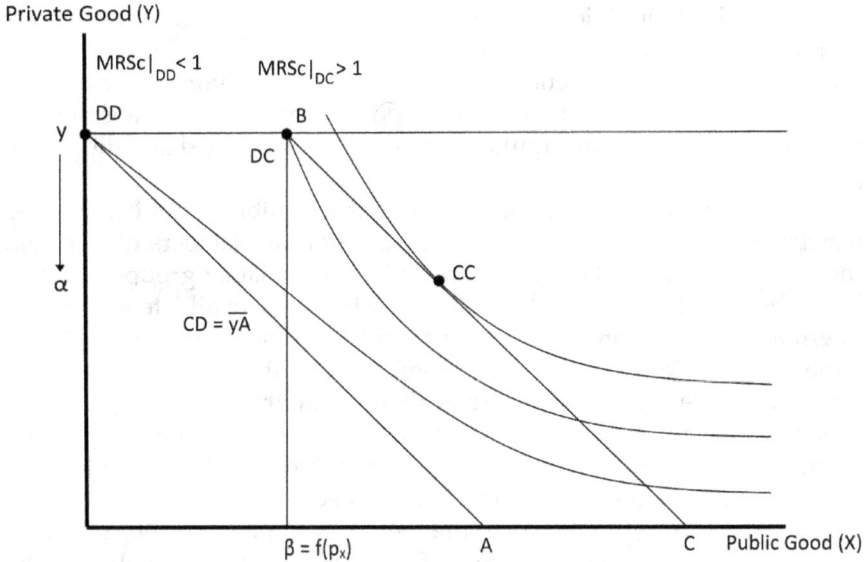

Figure 3.6. The assurance utility model (CC > DC > DD > CD). *Source:* author.

Private Good (Y)

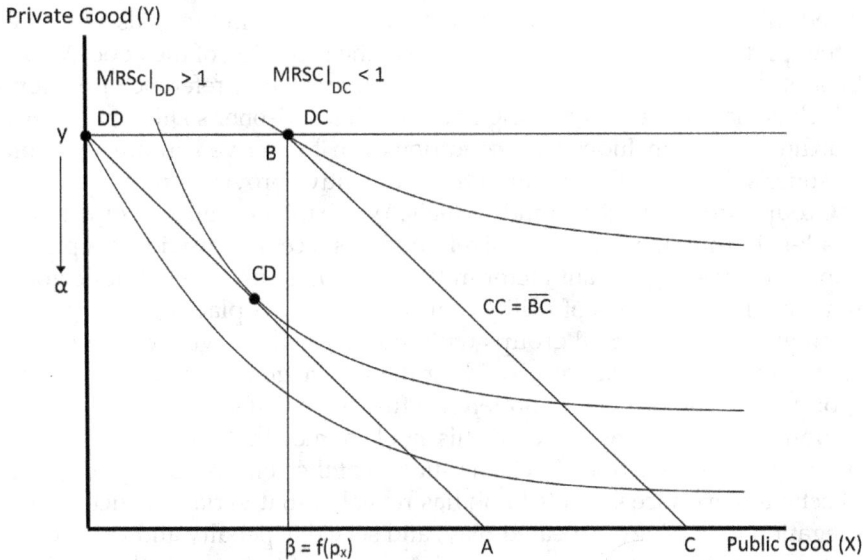

Figure 3.7. The chicken utility model (DC > CC > CD > DD). *Source:* author.

INDIVIDUAL PREFERENCE AND
THE COMPOSITION OF OLSON'S GROUPS

According to Olson (1971, 23–24 and 49–50), privileged groups have at least one member for whom the individual's utility from its supply of the good exceeds the individual's cost of contributing to the good. For goods that are not exceptionally lumpy, these individuals have a privileged or special privileged preference function and will therefore be willing to contribute some supply of the public good to its group even if it is the sole provider. Thus, as Olson stipulates, the group is privileged and the public good is supplied.

When the cost of individual provision of the public good exceeds the benefit of individual provision of the good for all members of a group, the group is latent. In Olson's typology of groups, latent groups can then be further classified by size.[11] Olson characterized a small latent group as intermediate where provision of the good is possible due primarily to the dynamics of interaction between members. Hardin (1982) asserted that total group size, N, is less important than the minimum size, k, of a sub-group whose members can benefit from their collective provision of the public good regardless of the participation of the rest of the latent group (i.e., the other N-k members). Hardin redefined the intermediate group as one where k is small rather than one where N is small. In the context of the present analysis, what preference function would the k members of the subgroup have? The members of this subgroup could not have either of the privileged preference functions or the group would be defined as a privileged group. No strategic interaction can motivate individuals with the latent preference function to participate in the provision of the good. Members of this k-subgroup must have the intermediate preference function, which is the preference ordering of the familiar Prisoner's Dilemma game. Hardin (1971) concludes that conditions can be derived in an n-person Prisoner's Dilemma that result in the cooperative provision of the good.

Groups are composed of individuals. While total group size or the size of a k-subgroup may affect the likelihood of success in providing a public good, the most significant factor in the decision to provide a public good remains the valuations of utility that the individual places on the public good and its costs. Small groups with members who have the latent preference function will fail at providing the public good as readily as large groups with the privileged preference functions will succeed.

Nothing that is presented in this book denies that the setting of the public goods interaction affects the success of the venture. Over fifty years of scholarship since Olson's book has revealed that variables such as aggregation technology, repeated play, and selective penalty and reward affect the provision of public goods. Since many of the models that explore these variables are based on the Prisoner's Dilemma, they are directly tied to the intermediate preference ordering proposed in this book. This book simply calls for a recognition that all public games decisions are ultimately derived from what the individual wants. Models that explore the effects of repeated play or aggregation technologies should first justify the individual's utilities for the public good and then show how interactions between these individuals are affected by the setting.

APPENDIX TO CHAPTER 3

List of Symbols

X	Quantity of public good
Y	Quantity of private good numeraire
y	Individual's endowment of private good numeraire
α	Quantity of private good numeraire the individual pays toward the supply of the public good. With a price ratio of 1:1, α is also the supply of public good provided by the individual.
β	Quantity of public good that the individual expects will be supplied by the rest of collective (not including the individual).
P_x	Individual's subjective probability that the collective will provide x units of public good.
$U_x(x)$	Individual's utility obtained from x units of public good, ceteris paribus.
$U_y(y)$	Individual's utility obtained from y units of private good, ceteris paribus.
$U_x(\alpha)$	Individual's utility obtained from its own supply of α units of public goods.
$U_x(\beta)$	Individual's utility obtained from the rest of the collective's supply of β units of public goods.
$U_x(\alpha+\beta)$	Individual's utility obtained from the joint supply of α units of public good by the individual plus β units of public goods by the rest of the collective.
$U_y(\alpha)$	Individual's utility lost by paying α units of private good to obtain α units of public good.
MRSc	The marginal rate of substitution in consumption. This rate measures the absolute value of the slope of an indifference curve. It is defined as U_x/U_y.
MRSc $|_{xy}$	The marginal rate of substitution in consumption evaluated at point xy.
$\Leftrightarrow$	Implies and is implied by.

Algebraic Proofs of Possible Preference Orderings
for the 2 x 2 Public Goods Games

In the following algebraic proofs, the values representing total utility of each outcome of the public goods decision are taken from the corresponding cells of figure 3.1.

Theorem 1: CC > CD

$\quad$ Proof: CC > CD $\quad\Leftrightarrow\quad$ $U_x(\alpha+\beta)+U_y(y-\alpha) > U_x(\alpha)+U_y(y-\alpha)$

$\qquad\qquad\qquad\quad\Leftrightarrow\quad$ $U_x(\alpha)+U_x(\beta) > U_x(\alpha)$

$\qquad\qquad\qquad\quad\Leftrightarrow\quad$ $U_x(\beta) > 0$ which is true by assumption, Q.E.D.

Theorem 1 states that the individual will always prefer collective provision to sole provision of the good. This is true because if $U_x(\beta)$ is positively valued, the individual will desire the additional value provided by the rest of the collective (β) above its own supply since there is no cost associated with the rest of the collective providing the good.

Theorem 2: CC > DC $\quad\Leftrightarrow\quad$ $U_x(\alpha) > U_y(\alpha)$

$\quad$ Proof: CC > DC $\quad\Leftrightarrow\quad$ $U_x(\alpha+\beta)+U_y(y-\alpha) > U_x(\beta)+U_y(y)$

$\qquad\qquad\qquad\quad\Leftrightarrow\quad$ $U_x(\alpha)+U_x(\beta)+U_y(y)-U_y(\alpha) > U_x(\beta)+U_y(y)$

$\qquad\qquad\qquad\quad\Leftrightarrow\quad$ $U_x(\alpha) > U_y(\alpha)$, Q.E.D.

The individual will prefer collective provision over free-riding if the utility of the supply provided by the individual exceeds the individual's cost of providing the good. In this case, the individual would prefer to participate in the provision of the good rather than forego the additional utility that it can provide itself.

Corollary 2.1: DC > CC $\Leftrightarrow U_y(\alpha) > U_x(\alpha)$ is proved by association.

Theorem 3: CC > DD $\quad\Leftrightarrow\quad$ $U_x(\alpha+\beta) > U_y(\alpha)$

$\quad$ Proof: CC > DD $\quad\Leftrightarrow\quad$ $U_x(\alpha+\beta)+U_y(y-\alpha) > U_y(y)$

$\qquad\qquad\qquad\quad\Leftrightarrow\quad$ $U_x(\alpha+\beta)+U_y(y)-U_y(\alpha) > U_y(y)$

$\qquad\qquad\qquad\quad\Leftrightarrow\quad$ $U_x(\alpha+\beta) > U_y(\alpha)$, Q.E.D.

Theorem 3 states that collective provision is preferred to no good being provided when the utility of the good supplied by the collective and the individual together is greater than the individual's cost of participating in the provision of the good.

Corollary 3.1: $DD > CC \Leftrightarrow U_y(\alpha) > U_x(\alpha+\beta)$ is proved by association.

Theorem 4: $CD > DC$ $\Leftrightarrow$ $U_x(\alpha)-U_y(\alpha) > U_x(\beta)$

      Proof: $CD > DC$ $\Leftrightarrow$ $U_x(\alpha)+U_y(y-\alpha) > U_x(\beta)+U_y(y)$

                       $\Leftrightarrow$ $U_x(\alpha)+U_y(y)-U_y(\alpha) > U_x(\beta)+U_y(y)$

                       $\Leftrightarrow$ $U_x(\alpha)-U_y(\alpha) > U_x(\beta)$, Q.E.D.

Sole provision of the good (CD) is preferred to free-riding (DC) when the net utility of the individual's contribution exceeds the utility gained from the public good provided by the rest of the collective. In this case the individual will be willing to provide the good by itself rather than forego the utility of its own supply by free-riding.

Corollary 4.1: $DC > CD \Leftrightarrow U_x(\beta) > U_x(\alpha)-U_y(\alpha)$. is proved by association.

Theorem 5: $CD > DD$ $\Leftrightarrow$ $U_x(\alpha) > U_y(\alpha)$

      Proof: $CD > DD$ $\Leftrightarrow$ $Ux(\alpha)+Uy(y-\alpha) > Uy(y)$

                       $\Leftrightarrow$ $U_x(\alpha)+U_y(y)-U_y(\alpha) > U_y(y)$

                       $\Leftrightarrow$ $U_x(\alpha) > U_y(\alpha)$, Q.E.D.

When the utility of the individual's supply of the good exceeds the cost of its supply, the individual will prefer to supply the good by itself over no good being supplied at all.

Corollary 5.1: $DD > CD \Leftrightarrow U_y(\alpha) > U_x(\alpha)$ is proved by association.

Theorem 6: $DC > DD$

      Proof: $DC > DD$ $\Leftrightarrow$ $Ux(\beta)+Uy(y) > Uy(y)$

                       $\Leftrightarrow$ $U_x(\beta) > 0$, which is true by assumption, Q.E.D.

Since the commodity is assumed to be a good ($U_x(\beta) > 0$), the individual will always prefer that someone else provide the good over no good being provided at all.

Theorem 7: CD > DD   ⇔   CC > DC

  Proof: CD > DD   ⇔   Ux(α) > Uy(α)   by Theorem 5

  $U_x(\alpha) > U_y(\alpha)$ ⇔   CC > DD   by Theorem 2, Q.E.D.

If the individual prefers sole provision to no good being provided it must perceive that the utility gained from its own supply of the good exceeds the costs incurred in providing the good. If this utility is greater than the costs, then the individual would logically prefer collective provision of the good to free-riding rather than forego the utility that its own supply would create.

Corollary 7.1: DD > CD ⇔   DC > CC

  Proof: DD > CD ⇔   Uy(α) > Ux(α)   by Corollary 5.1

  $U_y(\alpha) > U_x(\alpha)$ ⇔   DC > CC   by Corollary 2.1, Q.E.D.

Optimal Allocation between the Public and Private Goods

Optimal allocation for the individual between the public good (X) and the private good (Y) occurs in an interior solution when the Marginal Rate of Substitution in Consumption (MRSc) equals the Marginal Rate of Substitution in Exchange (MRSe). For an interior solution, this optimum will be at the point of tangency between the utility curve and one of the budget lines ($\overline{BC}$ and $\overline{yA}$) on the utility-based model, depending on the circumstance. The maximization problem is:

(1)   *Maximize $U_{(X,Y)}$ subject to $p_x X + p_y Y = y$*

The Lagrangian takes the form of:

(2)   *Maximize $L_{(x,y,\lambda)} = U(X,Y) - \lambda [p_x X + p_y Y - y]$*

The first order conditions for optimization are:

(3) $\dfrac{\partial L}{\partial \lambda} = p_x X + p_y Y - y = 0$

(4) $\dfrac{\partial L}{\partial X} = \dfrac{\partial U}{\partial X} - \lambda p_x = 0$

(5) $\dfrac{\partial L}{\partial Y} = \dfrac{\partial U}{\partial Y} - \lambda p_y = 0$

Conditions (4) and (5) imply equations (6) and (7):

(6) $$\dfrac{\partial U/\partial X}{p_x} = \dfrac{\partial U/\partial Y}{p_y}$$

(7) $$\dfrac{\partial U/\partial Y}{\partial U/\partial X} = \dfrac{p_y}{p_x} \rightarrow MRSc = MRSe$$

Equation (6) is the consumption balance equation. When the consumption balance equation is satisfied, the optimum allocation between X and Y will be an interior solution. (Hirshleifer 1980, 94–95). The optimum occurs where the Marginal Rate of Substitution in Consumption (MRSc) equals the Marginal rate of Consumption in Exchange (MRSe) as shown in equation (7). This occurs where one of the budget lines ($\bar{y}A$ or B^-C^-) is tangent to an indifferent curve. MRSc is the absolute value of the slope of an indifference curve at any point of tangency. MRSe is the absolute value of the budget line. Initially, MRSe = 1, by assumption.

When the consumption balance equation is not satisfied, the optimum is found in a corner solution. The marginal utility of a good divided by its price is the Marginal Utility per dollar spent (Hirshleifer 1980, 95). When the marginal utility per dollar spent of the public good is greater than the marginal utility per dollar spent of the private good, as in inequality (8), the MRSc (slope of the indifference curve at the corner solution) will be greater than 1 (inequality 9) and the indifference curve will intersect the endowment line below the budget line as it does at the DD and DC outcomes in the Special Privileged and Privileged preference orderings.

(8) $$\dfrac{\partial U/\partial X \,(x=0)}{p_x} > \dfrac{\partial U/\partial Y \,(Y>0)}{p_y} \quad (X=0,\ Y=y)$$

(9) $$\dfrac{\partial U/\partial Y}{\partial U/\partial X} > \dfrac{p_y}{p_x} \quad (X=0, Y=y)$$

Thus, outcomes that lie along the joint provision line $\overline{BC}$ and along the sole provision line $\overline{yA}$ in the indifference graphs will be preferred to free-riding (DC) and no provision (DD) respectively.

When the marginal utility per dollar spent of the public good is less than the marginal utility per dollar spent of the private good, as in inequality (10), the MRSc will be less than 1 (see inequality 11) and the indifference curve will intersect the endowment line above the budget line as it does at the DD and DC outcomes in the Intermediate and Latent preference orderings.

$$(10) \quad \frac{\partial U / \partial X \, (x = 0)}{p_x} < \frac{\partial U / \partial Y \, (Y > 0)}{p_y} \quad (X = 0, Y = y)$$

$$(11) \quad \frac{\partial U / \partial Y}{\partial U / \partial X} < \quad (X = 0, Y = y)$$

In the Intermediate and Latent preference orderings, free-riding (DC) and no provision ($\underline{DD}$) will be preferred to outcomes that lie along the joint provision line $\overline{BC}$ and along the sole provision line $\overline{yA}$ in the indifference graphs, respectively.

Necessary and Sufficient Conditions for the Preference Orderings

The necessary and sufficient conditions for each of the four preference orderings can be derived from the preference relations embedded in Theorems 1 through Corollary 7.1. If the net benefit of the individual's provision of the public good is greater than the benefit of the good provided by the rest of the collective, then the individual will have the Special Privileged preference ordering.

Theorem 8: $U_x(\alpha) - U_y(\alpha) > U_x(\beta) \Leftrightarrow CC > CD > DC > DD$
      Proof: $U_x(\alpha) - U_y(\alpha) > U_x(\beta) \Leftrightarrow CD > DC$ by Theorem 4
                $CC > CD$ by Theorem 1
                $DC > DD$ by Theorem 6
                $CC > CD$ and $CD > DC$ and $DC > DD \Leftrightarrow CC > CD > DC > DD$,
                by Transitivity, Q.E.D.

If the benefit of the public good provided by the individual is greater than the cost of the individual's provision *and* the benefit of the public good provided by the rest of the collective is greater than the net benefit of the individual's provision (benefit - cost) then the individual will have the Privileged preference ordering.

Theorem 9: $[U_x(\alpha) > U_y(\alpha) \ \& \ U_x(\beta) > U_x(\alpha) - U_y(\alpha)] \Leftrightarrow CC > DC > CD > DD$

  Proof: $U_x(\alpha) > U_y(\alpha) \Leftrightarrow CC > DC$ by Theorem 2

  $U_x(\beta) > U_x(\alpha) - U_y(\alpha) \Leftrightarrow DC > CD$ by Corollary 4.1

  $U_x(\alpha) > U_y(\alpha) \Leftrightarrow CD > DD$ by Theorem 5

  $CC > DC$ and $DC > CD$ and $CD > DD \Leftrightarrow CC > DC > CD > DD$,
  by transitivity, Q.E.D.

If the benefit of joint provision of the public good is greater than the individual's cost of providing the public good *and* the benefit of sole provision of the good is greater than the individual's cost of providing the public good, then the individual will have the Intermediate preference ordering.

Theorem 10: $[U_x(\alpha+\beta) > U_y(\alpha) \ \& \ U_y(\alpha) > U_x(\alpha)] \Leftrightarrow DC > CC > DD > CD$

  Proof: $U_y(\alpha) > U_x(\alpha) \Leftrightarrow DC > CC$ by Corollary 2.1

  $U_x(\alpha+\beta) > U_y(\alpha) \Leftrightarrow CC > DD$ by Theorem 3

  $U_y(\alpha) > U_x(\alpha) \Leftrightarrow DD > CD$ by Corollary 5.1

  $DC > CC$ and $CC > DD$ and $DD > CD \Leftrightarrow DC > CC > DD > CD$
  by transitivity, Q.E.D.

If the cost of the individual contributing the public good is greater than the benefit of joint provision of the public good, then the individual will have the Latent preference ordering.

Theorem 11: $U_y(\alpha) > U_x(\alpha+\beta) \Leftrightarrow DC > DD > CC > DC$

  Proof: $U_y(\alpha) > U_x(\alpha+\beta) \Leftrightarrow DD > CC$ by Corollary 3.1

  $DC > DD$ by Theorem 6

  $CC > CD$ by Theorem 1

  $DC > DD$ and $DD > CC$ and $CC > CD \Leftrightarrow DC > DD > CC > CD$
  by transitivity, Q.E.D.

NOTES

1. The three categories of literature discussed here follow the categories of Olson's propositions identified by Sandler (2015, 199) in his review of fifty years of scholarship since *The Logic of Collective Action*.

2. The private good numeraire can be money, time, in-kind services, or anything else the individual values. The point is that contributing to the provision of a public good is costly.

3. This assumption means that the production function (or budget line) on a utility graph will be linear with a slope of -1. This assumption will make the following specification of the individual's preferences easier to explain. Relaxation of this assumption will affect the mathematics of the marginal rate of substitution

conditions developed later but will have no effect on the conclusions drawn from this analysis.

4. The quantity β is the individual's expected value of the amount of public good that will be provided by the rest of the collective. It is a function of the individual's subjective probability that the rest of the collective will provide various amounts of the public good. Thus $\beta = \Sigma p_x X$, where p_x is the individual's subjective probability that the rest of the collective will provide X units of public goods.

5. In the graphical analysis that follows, this assumption means that the slopes of all indifference curves are equal along the horizontal line at y through the graph.

6. This method of using indifference analysis is based on Samuelson's (1955) criteria for the optimal individual provision of public goods. For examples of similar methods see Buchanan (1968); Fogarty (1981); Lichbach (1992); Sandler (1992); Shibata (1971) and Taylor (1976).

7. Ux and Uy are partial derivatives of the individual's utility function with respect to x and y. Graphically, along an indifference curve, $0 = d U = Ux_x + Uy_y$, indicating that utility remains constant along any given indifference curve. The absolute value of the slope of an indifference curve with respect to x and y is the marginal rate of substitution in consumption (MRSc) and is commonly denoted as Ux/Uy. See Hirshleifer (1980, 74–75, especially the mathematical footnotes) and Chiang (1974, 391–392).

8. As seen on figures 3.2–3.5, the four utility models are distinguished by the relative steepness or flatness of the indifference curves. The absolute value of the slope of the indifference curve at any point is the marginal rate of substitution in consumption (MRSc) at that point. For the privileged and special privileged preference functions, the MRSc $|_{DC>1}$, indicating steeper slopes in the indifference curves. For the intermediate and latent utility models, the MRSc $|_{DC \leq 1}$, indicating flatter slopes in the indifference curves.

9. Another example that fits the special privileged preference ordering is cited by Hardin (1982, 42). Billionaire Howard Hughes bought a Las Vegas television station in the days before VHS, DVD, Blu-Ray or streaming services to ensure that he could watch western and aviation movies between midnight and 6 am thus providing this "good" to hundreds of thousands of others.

10. Sandler (1992, 40) also uses this preference ordering to represent a "fully privileged" group member.

11. Hardin (1982, 40) described Olson's typology as two "parallel typologies" —one based on "an analytical (or economic) argument that divides *all groups* into privileged and latent categories," and one based on "empirical (or political-sociological) arguments that divide *latent groups* into smaller and larger categories" (emphasis in the original).

FOUR

Leadership and the Global Monetary System

INTERNATIONAL MONETARY MANAGEMENT AS A GLOBAL PUBLIC GOOD

It is easy to portray the global response to the West African Ebola epidemic in 2014 as a global public good. It was non-excludable because stopping the epidemic benefitted all countries whether they paid for it or not. It was indivisible because benefits of stopping the disease are not consumed. The benefits extended to people in all socio-economic groups and whether or not the disease returns, the benefits of the response are inter-generational from the lessons learned about treatment and containment. It may not be as easy to see management of the international economy as a global public good. The similarities between responding to an epidemic and managing the economy, however, are significant. In both cases, the benefits accrue, not so much from what the actions create, as from what they prevent. Curbing a local epidemic before it becomes a worldwide pandemic reduces the threat that those distant from its original source will be affected. Managing the world economy to prevent a national recession from becoming a worldwide depression also reduces the threat that those distant from the original event will be affected. President Roosevelt made this point in his message to the delegates to the United Nations Monetary and Financial Conference at Bretton Woods, New Hampshire on July 1, 1944.

> Economic diseases are highly communicable. It follows, therefore, that the economic health of every country is a proper matter of concern to all its neighbors, near and distant. Only through a dynamic and soundly expanding world economy can the living standards of individual nations be advanced to levels which will permit a full realization of our hopes and future. (*New York Times* 1944a, 14)

Charles Wyplosz (1999, 156) noted that "financial stability can be seen as an international public good because financial instability is a potential

49

public bad that spreads across countries." Financial crises are certainly unwanted, non-excludable, and indivisible, making them public bads. National financial crises become global financial crises due to spillover effects when international markets transmit national market failures around the world and due to races to the bottom when national authorities intervene to correct market failures causing authorities in other states to follow suit with even more drastic measures. (Wyplosz 1999, 159–160).

If financial instability is a global public bad, does it necessarily follow that policies to create international financial stability are global public goods? Charles Kindleberger (1981, 247) claimed that "The analysis of public and private goods is also applicable to the international economy. For private goods, read national benefits, and for public, cosmopolitan goods, for the maintenance of the world economy." [1] Whether management of the global economy is a public good or not depends on two factors. The first factor involves power. Providing a public good can be costly, especially when there are many free-riders, but in international affairs it can also create effects that benefit only the provider in highly asymmetrical relationships. Charles Kindleberger recognized this when he stated that

> Management of the gold-exchange standard by Britain from 1870 to 1913 and by the United States from 1945 to 1971 can be viewed as provision of either the public good of international money, or the private good for itself of seigniorage, which is the profit that comes to the seigneur, or sovereign power, from the issuance of money. (Kindleberger 1981, 248)

In theory, the motives of a supplier of a good should not matter, but if there are spin-off consequences of consuming a public good, then the good can become a bad. One such consequence of any international economic transaction is the effect that asymmetric benefits from the transaction can have on long-term relations between the parties. Albert Hirschman discussed the problems of asymmetric benefits in his study of trade between Germany and the states of Southern Europe prior to World War II. He identified two effects on the power of a state that derive from trade. The supply effect occurs when "providing a more plentiful supply of goods or by replacing goods wanted less by goods wanted more (from the power standpoint), enhances the potential military force of a country" (Hirschman 1945, 14). This is the classic economic justification for trade. In a realist, mercantilist world, Hirschman noted that any increase in wealth through the supply effect increases the relative power of a country. More interesting to the present analysis is Hirschman's discussion of the influence effect of trade. The influence effect occurs when Country A's opportunity cost of stopping trade with Country B is prohibitively high. This gives Country B power over Country A by threatening to cut off or restrict trade.

Concerns over the influence effects of trade with the United States after the war formed a sub-text for the issues raised by the smaller countries during the Bretton Woods conference. The American delegation, in an effort to quell domestic opposition, predicted that U.S. exports would triple under the Bretton Woods arrangements (Crider 1944a). The Peruvian delegation called for the creation of an international trade agreement to accompany the discussions related to the International Monetary Fund and the World Bank. The delegation even threatened that if trade matters were not taken up soon, they would "be bound to develop such disruptive tendencies as might be capable of wrecking any plan" (Crider 1944b). John Maynard Keynes tried to respond to the British House of Lords concerns about the scale of U.S. exports by noting that the guiding principles that were developed for the Bretton Woods required that "a proper share of responsibility for maintaining equilibrium in the balance of international payments is squarely placed on the creditor countries" (Crider 1944a).

Fears of the asymmetric structure of the postwar economy and of the administration of the Bretton Woods institutions were well founded. After the war devastated much of the world's productive capacity, the United States clearly had the most powerful economy. Wartime lending meant that the United States had acquired nearly 70 percent of the world's gold supply (IMF 2001). In 1950, the United States produced 27.3 percent of the total world Gross Domestic Product (GDP) compared to only 26.2 percent produced by all the countries of Western Europe. (Maddison 2007, 381). The United States also held the most voting power in the Bretton Woods institutions. The original Articles of Agreement of the IMF allotted voting power by the size of the member state's subscription quota. Article XII, Section 5 established the voting power of each member as 250 votes plus 1 vote for every $100,000 of the member's IMF quota. The United States initially held 28.0 percent of the total voting power in the institution. This was more than the voting power of all the countries in Africa, Asia, Latin America, and the Middle East combined (IMF 1944, 42).

The second factor that affects whether management of the economy is a global public good is the degree of collateral damage that management efforts create. The protests in the early 2000s against the International Monetary Fund's (IMF) structural adjustment programs highlighted how efforts to manage the macro economy could cause negative externalities among local populations. Scott Barrett (2007, 167) emphasized this by stating that "We should not be surprised that only *some* global public goods help the worst-off people, for few, if any, are provided specifically for this purpose . . . global public goods are usually provided by and for the better-off countries" (emphasis in the original). While the benefits of structural adjustment as a good are mixed, the social cost can be high.

Hartzell et al. (2010) found that these programs can increase domestic tensions that lead to an increased incidence of civil war. Abouharb and Cingranelli (2006) found that structural adjustment programs can worsen human rights abuses, including torture, political imprisonment, extra-judicial killing, and disappearances.

Yet the fact remains that financial instability can be a global public bad. A program that promotes financial stability is a global public good if it provides sufficient benefits that outweigh any influence effect of provision of the good and if it does not create substantial collateral damage to local populations. The management of the international monetary system by the United States of America from 1944 through 1971 seems to meet these two criteria. While the United States did benefit from seigniorage as the provider of the world currency, that benefit diminished rapidly as the postwar economies of Europe and Japan recovered from the war. The United States of America continued to provide the global public good of monetary stabilization long after the seigniorage benefit waned. The structure of the postwar economy provided the United States with substantial supply and influence effects from the policies to manage the international economy and the United States used this power to dominate its relations with other states. However, the benefits from monetary management were generalized in preventing financial crises and did not create the same level of local collateral damage that was later caused by IMF structural adjustment programs.

This chapter examines the United States' role in managing the global monetary system between 1945 and 1971 using a utility-based model of public goods. The goal is to document changing preferences for supplying the public good of financial management due to changing U.S. identities during that period. I begin with a brief discussion of public goods and the history of monetary management. I then analyze the development of U.S. identities and U.S. behavior in the monetary system from 1945 through 1971, using the utility-based model.

INTERNATIONAL MONETARY MANAGEMENT 1945–1971

The devastation of World War II extended well beyond the estimated 50 to 70 million human casualties. Europe lost approximately 70 percent of its industrial infrastructure in the war. (Pilisuk and Roundtree 2008, 136). The postwar economies suffered massive inflation. In 1948 prices in Austria were 200 percent higher than they were in 1939 and prices in France were 1,820 percent higher (International Monetary Fund 2001). To address these and other economic issues arising from the destruction of World War II, the United States hosted representatives of forty-four states at the United Nations Monetary and Financial Conference at the Mount Washington Hotel in Bretton Woods, New Hampshire on July 1, 1944.[2] "For the first time ever, governments were formally committing themselves to the principle of collective responsibility for management of the international monetary system" (Cohen 1977, 93). Bretton Woods also created the International Bank for Reconstruction and Development (IBRD), later known as the World Bank, to provide loans for postwar recovery.

The Bretton Woods system was not sufficient to deal with the need for postwar recovery. Too few members of the IMF were able to meet their subscription quotas and the funds donated by the United States to the IBRD were simply not enough. The IBRD relied on commercial banks to float bonds, which forced IBRD into a conservative lending pattern that many recovering states could not meet (Spero and Hart 1997, 11). Within two years of its implementation, the Bretton Woods system was collapsing.

In 1947, the United States stepped in to stabilize the monetary system. The wartime devastation of Europe and Japan coupled with the strength of the U.S. economy and the U.S. security commitments in the face of a rising Soviet threat made U.S. leadership acceptable abroad and at home (Spero and Hart 2010, 16–17; and Helleiner 1994, 67–72). According to Barry Eichengreen (2011, 6), the conventional wisdom that a strong currency makes a nation-state strong is wrong. Rather, it is a state's status as a great power that makes its money an international currency. "A currency is attractive because the country issuing it is large, rich, and growing. It is attractive because the country standing behind it is powerful and secure." In the direct aftermath of World War II, only the United States could claim great power status. The dollar became the world's currency and the United States maintained its value against gold at $35 per ounce. To counter a shortage of dollars on the world markets, the United States began a series of programs that pumped dollars into the global economy. The largest of these was the Marshall Plan that provided $17 billion in grants to European countries between 1948 and 1952 (Spero and Hart 2010, 17). Through the Marshall Plan, direct military assistance to many allied countries, and payments related to the Korean War, the United States maintained a balance of payments deficit from 1947 through 1958, ensuring a steady flow of dollars into the world markets. Such policies might have harmed the U.S. domestic economy had it not been for its incredible postwar strength. The United States, however, preferred to recreate and maintain a strong global market even if it meant weakening its domestic markets.

In effect, what the United States did was to abjure any payments target of its own in favor of taking responsibility for operation of the monetary order itself. Other countries set independent balance-of-payments targets; America's external financial policy was essentially one of "benign neglect." Consistency in monetary relations was ensured not by multilateral cooperation but by America's willingness to play a passive role in the adjustment process . . . The growth of the world's liquidity supply was largely determined, consequently, by the magnitude of America's deficits—modified only to the extent that these deficits were settled in gold, rather than dollars, reflecting the asset preferences of surplus countries. (Cohen 1977, 96)

The resulting monetary system became "a hegemonic monetary order centered on the dollar" (Cohen 1977, 96) with the United States as the hegemonic leader. The United States provided liquidity in the form of grants and aid. It stabilized currency by allowing foreign currencies to be converted to dollars at their par exchange rates that could be readily converted to gold through the U.S. open gold window.

The system worked. By 1958, the major economies of Europe and Japan were nearly fully recovered. Balance of payments had improved and gold reserves in Europe and Japan equaled those in the United States (Spero and Hart 2010, 17). By this time the U.S. domestic interests were beginning to lose their taste for running balance of payments deficits. Due to the successful policies at the beginning of the decade to pump dollars into the system, by the end of the 1950s the world was experiencing a dollar glut and some economists were speculating that the dollar was overvalued. This sentiment was exacerbated by an influential proposal by Princeton University economist Robert Triffin (1960), dubbed "the Triffin Dilemma."

- A monetary system based on one country's currency requires that the host country pump its currency into the system to create liquidity by running a *balance of payment deficit.*
- As the volume of the currency circulating abroad increases, it becomes overvalued creating a lack of confidence in the system.
- To rebuild confidence in the system without devaluing its primary medium of exchange, the host country must run a *balance of payments surplus.*

The crisis for the dollar came in the fall of 1960 when private speculation on the London gold market drove the price of gold to $40 per ounce. This caused a run to the United States to buy gold at the pegged rate of $35 per ounce at a time when dollars abroad exceeded the value of the U.S. gold reserves (Zimmerman 2002, 111). The bulk of the crisis came after November 8, 1960, when John F. Kennedy was elected to be the next president. A lame duck President Eisenhower faced his last foreign policy crisis. Eisenhower recognized the importance of linking the U.S. balance of payments to threatening to reduce the U.S. military presence in Europe. This would have the dual benefit of reducing U.S. payments abroad and providing a lever for negotiations with a security conscious Europe. In a letter on October 31, Eisenhower asked Chancellor Adenauer of West Germany to provide more funding to NATO and to pick up some of the cost of U.S. troops stationed in Europe (*New York Times* 1960a). In response, Adenauer requested a high-level meeting of U.S. and German experts. The United States sent Robert Anderson, secretary of the treasury, and C. Douglas Dillon, under secretary of state, to meet with officials in Bonn, Paris, and London in mid-November. Upon returning, Anderson and Dillon reported that Adenauer repeatedly indicated that his greatest fear was that the United States would redeploy the troops. Anderson maintained that veiled threat, stating that, "the President will do anything necessary to protect the dollar" (U.S. Department of State 1960). Although the Anderson-Dillon trip failed to get any significant concessions from the European allies, it was a turning point in U.S. management of the monetary system, for it signaled that the United States desired to reduce its role as the sole manager of the monetary policy but the United States still wanted to maintain the integrity of the dollar system.

> The first run on the dollar, which occurred in November 1960 . . . signaled the end of the unilateral system of U.S. management. The dollar system did not collapse. The United States was still able to play a strong leadership role and the dollar and its economy remained healthy. But the United States could no longer manage the system alone. Henceforth, it would be obliged to join in the collective management, to seek the cooperation of other members of the system, and to make concessions. (Spero and Hart 2010, 18)

The gold crisis of 1960 caused a significant change in U.S. priorities and preferences. Beginning in 1961, management of the monetary system turned from U.S. hegemony to multilateral management. Although the system was still grounded in the dollar backed by gold, the IMF began to play a greater role in creating the liquidity of the system and the U.S. Federal Reserve began attending meetings of the Bank of International Settlements (BIS) in Basel. The real shift to multilateral management came in December, 1961 with the creation of the Group of Ten.[3] The Group of Ten created a $6 billion fund under its control to be used to manage monetary problems. Other management mechanisms instituted by the group included a two-tier gold market where private sales could fluctuate with the market while official sales were kept at $35 per ounce to support the dollar, a currency swap system, standby credit lines to be used for crisis management, and U.S. bonds denominated in foreign currencies that could be held in reserve in lieu of gold (Spero and Hart 2010, 19).

The multilateral management system worked well until 1971 when, once again, there was a run on gold as the perception that the now excessive stock of dollars circulating in the world was overvalued. This was exacerbated by substantial inflation in the United States and the effect of the Vietnam War on the U.S. economy. On August 15, 1971, President Nixon, without consulting the European allies, announced that the U.S. gold window was closed. The dollar could no longer be converted to gold (Nixon 1971). This marked the end of the Bretton Woods period and it marked a significant shift in U.S. priorities and preferences for providing monetary stabilization (Spero and Hart 2010, 24).

Agents in the international system (people, states, corporations, NGOs, etc.) construct their own identities based on their needs and the contingencies of their situation. Agents also have identities constructed for them. In either case, identities are more than descriptive; they are also performative. Identities establish the interests of the agents and establish rules of behavior relevant to those interests. To say that the United States took on the identity of hegemonic leader of the global monetary system in 1947 is to place the United States in a whole nexus of political and social relations that is sometimes referred to as hegemonic stability theory.

The logic of hegemonic stability is relatively straightforward. Generalized growth and prosperity in the capitalist international economy require open competition and free trade. While these conditions may be advantageous for the collective of world economies, the policies that are necessary to create and maintain an open international economy, such as removal of barriers to trade, may be detrimental to the well-being of individual economies. Since it may be in the collective interest to create and maintain an open world economy but not in the interest of individual agents to pursue policies that will do so, the order will not be created without the influence of a hegemon that is willing and able to forego short term individual interests in favor of greater utility gained from the open economy.

Kindleberger (1981, 247) believed the hegemon created stability by providing an import market for goods when international demand fell, providing a steady flow of capital even when business cycles turn toward investment contraction, and providing and maintaining the value of the primary currency for foreign exchange. The conclusion of hegemonic stability theory is that a stable, open, international economy can only occur when a large powerful state provides hegemonic leadership. Supporters of the theory point to two empirical examples—the British hegemony of the nineteenth century and the American hegemony of the period following World War II. The corollary of the theory is that the international economy becomes unstable when no state rises to the task of hegemonic leadership. Supporters of the theory can point to the period following World War I when, in the absence of a hegemonic leadership, the European system fell into nationalistic trade wars that led to the Great Depression and ultimately to World War II. The theory is less able to explain the stability of the international economy that persisted after the American hegemony waned in the last quarter of the twentieth century.

Hegemonic stability theory became the target of significant critique and even derision in the 1990s and the early twenty-first century. That a stable international economy persisted after U.S. hegemony calls into question whether stability was a function of hegemonic leadership or American economic power. Both Great Britain and the United States were success-ful at stabilizing the economy but neither was successful at liberalizing the economy.

Although my analysis does examine American management of the international monetary system between 1945 and 1971, it does not rely on hegemonic stability theory. My analysis neither implies that monetary stabilization requires the action of a hegemon nor does it imply that the absence of a hegemon leads to instability. This analysis merely notes that the United States did take on the identity of a hegemonic leader after World War II to provide the public good of monetary stabilization and asks why a state would do this in the face of free-riders and necessary compromises that may hurt its own economic position. The answer, I believe, is found in the relationship between a state's socially constructed identity in the international system and the preferences for the public good that are generated by that identity. The problem of creating and maintaining global monetary stability remains a problem of collective action to provide a public good, regardless of the validity of hegemonic stability theory.

U.S. PREFERENCES FOR MANAGING THE MONETARY SYSTEM: 1945–1971 AND BEYOND

The utility-based model of public goods presented in chapter 3 can be used to explain the preferences of the United States for providing the global public good of monetary management in the postwar period. The Bretton Woods agreement provided hope for recovery but in 1945, most of the world was not in any shape to implement it. Very few states were able to meet their subscription obligations and the war-torn economies could not commit their currencies to convertibility (Cohen 1977, 94–95). From 1945 through 1960, the United States stepped into the leadership role to provide the global public good of monetary management because it preferred the benefit of a stabilized system over the cost of managing the system, even it if had to pay all of those costs. Immediately after World War II, the United States' preference for the public good conformed to the special privileged preferences discussed in chapter 3. Once the European economies began to recover, the United States began to feel the burden of the dollar glut. The November 1960 run on the U.S. gold reserves shifted the U.S. preferences for managing the monetary system slightly to conform with the privileged preferences discussed above. The United States was still willing to cover the cost of stabilization, but its benefits from the system were reduced and it was looking for ways to shift the costs to other states. The dramatic change in U.S. preferences for providing monetary stabilization came in 1971, when recessionary and inflationary pressures combined with the ongoing expenditures related to the Vietnam War pushed President Nixon to close the gold window. At this point the U.S. preferences for the public good of managing the monetary shifted again, this time to the intermediate preference structure.

European preferences for providing the public good of a stable monetary system were also shifting. From 1945 to 1958, the capitalist economies other than the United States and Canada may have wanted a stabilized monetary system, but they were in no position to contribute to its costs. Their preference for this public good aligned with the latent preference ordering of the last section. Most of the major European currencies returned to convertibility in 1958, which signaled an increased preference for maintaining the monetary system, but they were not so strong as to be able to pay for the public good on their own. By the late 1950s these countries' preferences for the public good conformed to the intermediate preference ordering.

The U.S. preferences for a stable monetary system were driven by two factors after World War II. The world economic system was in shambles after the war. The U.S. economy, however, was at its highest production capacity, due to the exceptional production capacity that was developed to support the war effort. The United States was ramped up and ready to sell but it had no buyers because of the devastation of its trading partners during the war. A stabilized monetary system was the first step toward normalizing world demand for U.S. products. The second factor that contributed to U.S. preferences for a stable monetary system was the desire to build a military and economic defense against a strengthening Soviet Union. Economic woes breed discontent and discontent opens the doors for political strife that could challenge the capitalist-democratic regimes. As Marina Whitman stated:

> The need to maximize the economic strength of free-world nations as part of a bulwark against the perceived threat of Communist aggression underlay domestic support for Marshall Plan aid, for subsequent security arrangements in Europe, and for economic aid to developing countries . . . Everyone

accepted chronic U.S. payments deficits and a dollar-centered international monetary system as yet another aspect of the security umbrella. (Whitman 1975, 139–140)

The special privileged preference ordering values joint provision of the public good (CC) above all other outcomes, but it also values sole provision (CD) over free-riding (DC). This preference ordering can only come about if the agent perceives the value of its own contribution of the public good higher than any amount the agent perceives that the rest of the collective will contribute if the agent free-rides (DC > CD). This preference graph is shown in figure 3.2. The steepness of the indifference curves with respect to the quantity of the public good indicates the agent's strong preference for the public good over a private good numeraire. While the other capitalist economies desired a stable monetary system, they were in no position to contribute anything to its creation or management. Their preferences for the public good conformed to the latent preference ordering illustrated in figure 3.5. Quite the opposite of the special privileged preferences, the flatness of the latent indifference curves shows these agents would rather have no public good if they have to contribute to its provision (DD > CD). They only desire the public good if someone else provides it and they can free-ride. This combination of preferences creates the public goods interaction game shown in figure 4.1.[4]

Other Countries

United States	Do Not Contribute Good (D)	Contribute Good (C)
Do Not Contribute Good (D)	1, 3	2, 1
Contribute Good (C)	[3, 4] *	4, 2 *

Figure 4.1. Public Goods Game for Monetary Management—1945 to 1958. United States: Special Privileged Preferences; Others: Intermediate Preferences. *Source:* author.

The outcome of the game in figure 4.1 would be for the United States to contribute to the public good while the other countries free-ride. Both players have dominant strategies (row: C; column: D). Rapoport and Guyer (1966) classify the game as a stable equilibrium game (#14), meaning that if the United States either threatened to stop managing the monetary system or actually stopped managing the system, the other countries would not move to provide the public good. This game provides a good model of the history of this period when only the United States had the resources and the will to manage the monetary system.

The European and Japanese economies had substantially recovered by 1958. Most of the major European currencies returned to convertibility and European states began to meet their subscriptions to the IMF. U.S. preferences for the public good remained constant through this period but, as currencies returned to convertibility, the other countries' preferences for monetary management shifted to the intermediate preference ordering as shown in figure 3.4. The indifference curves in figure 3.4 are steeper with regard to the public good. Free-riding is still preferred to cooperative provision (DC > CC) but the agents now prefer to contribute to the good cooperatively rather than have no stabilization be provided (CC > DD). This leads to the strategic interaction game shown in figure 4.2.

Other Countries

United States	Do Not Contribute Good (D)	Contribute Good (C)
Do Not Contribute Good (D)	1, 2	2, 1
Contribute Good (C)	[3, 4] *	4, 3 *

Figure 4.2. Public Goods Game for Monetary Management—1958 to 1961. United States: Special Privileged Preferences; Others: Intermediate Preferences. *Source:* author.

The outcome of the game is, again, that the United States provided the management of the monetary system while the rest of the countries were free-riders. There are, however, subtle differences from the earlier game. This game is classified in Rapoport and Guyer's taxonomy as a threat vulnerable game (#19), which means that if the United States threatened to discontinue its management policies, the other countries would be willing to cooperate in providing monetary stability. While the United States did not explicitly threaten to end its stabilization policies at this time, it did become concerned with the effect the rising deficits was having on the U.S. economy. Hubert Zimmerman (2002, 106) noted,

> In November 1958 President Eisenhower and Robert Anderson informed the Senate majority leader, Lyndon B. Johnson, about warnings from abroad concerning the dollar's stability. Eisenhower set the tone of the later debate stating that "the stability of our currency is an absolute necessity to our security and our economic development," but serious discussion started only in mid-1959.

U.S. preferences for managing the monetary system shifted again after the gold crisis in November 1960. The U.S. balance of payments deficit in 1958 grew to 3.6 billion and grew even larger in 1959 and 1960 (Cohen 1977, 98). The dollar shortage of the early 1950s was now a dollar glut and many analysts were beginning to see the dollar as overvalued. This shook confidence in the dollar and led to the run on gold in November 1960. In 1951, the United States held 65.4 percent of the world's gold supply. By 1961, that percentage dropped to 48.4 percent (World Gold Council 2011). Although the gold crisis of 1960 shook the U.S. economy, the United States still desired to contribute to the public good of monetary management. A subtle change shifted the U.S. preferences for the public good of monetary management from the special privileged preference ordering shown in figure 3.2 to the privileged preference ordering shown in figure 3.3. The flatter indifference curves mean that U.S. preferences moved away from the public good toward the private good numeraire. The United States now preferred free-riding to sole provision of the good (DC > DC). The resulting public goods game is shown in figure 4.3.

Other Countries

United States	Do Not Contribute Good (D)	Contribute Good (C)
Do Not Contribute Good (D)	1, 2	3, 1
Contribute Good (C)	[2, 4] *	4, 3 *

Figure 4.3. Public Goods Game for Monetary Management—1961 to 1971. United States: Privileged Preferences; Others: Intermediate Preferences. *Source*: author.

The outcome of this game is still that the United States provides the system stabilization while the rest of the countries free-ride. The game is threat vulnerable in Rapoport and Guyer's taxonomy (#21). This time, the United States made use of the threat vulnerability. When Secretary of the Treasury Robert Anderson and Under Secretary of State C. Douglas Dillon met with Germany's Chancellor Adenauer in November, 1960, Adenauer made it clear that Germany did not want the United States to redeploy troops to resolve its balance of payments problems. Anderson and Dillon pressed this point to their advantage as documented in a memorandum that recorded their meeting with President Eisenhower upon their return.

> Again, and again Chancellor Adenauer came back to the point that there is only one thing that worries him, and that is the possibility that we might redeploy some of our troops. On this point, Secretary Anderson stated and reiterated that President Eisenhower is resolved to do whatever the United States has to do to protect the dollar. (U.S. Department of State 1960)

The Anderson-Dillon trip did not result in any significant contribution to managing the monetary system, so the United States moved to strengthen the threat of troop redeployment. One step was to reduce the number of dependents of military personnel abroad that the United States supported from 484,000 to 200,000. In a news conference on November 17, Eisenhower responded to a question about troop withdrawal by asserting:

> Well, I think we should never want to reduce our forces so far that people would think we had abandoned the area, or we had lowered our flag in that area. Not at all, but I do think that the time is coming when all of us will have to study very carefully what should be our proper portion of the load. (*New York Times* 1960b)

The administration gently continued to push the threat of troop redeployment:

> There was much debate over whether the United States should announce such a reduction at the NATO Council ministerial meeting in December 1960. It was finally decided to introduce the following sentence into a speech that State Secretary Herter gave to the meeting: "Some redeployment may become necessary unless our balance of payments can be brought into a more reasonable equilibrium." (Zimmerman 2002, 117).

The result of these threats was that the other countries and institutions began to take a more active role in providing the public good of managing the monetary system. Monetary management shifted from the hegemony of the United States to a number of multilateral forums. With increased quotas producing more funds, the IMF took a greater role in lending to European states that needed temporary relief for balance of payments problems. The United States began to participate in the meetings of the European Bank for International Settlements (BIS) in Basel, which allowed the BIS to have more control over the monetary system. Finally, the Group of Ten was created in 1961 where finance ministers from large industrial economies could meet to address monetary issues. The United States continued to provide a substantial share of the management of the monetary system through the 1960s by ensuring the convertibility of the dollar to gold. However, it effectively used the threat vulnerability of the interaction between its privileged preferences and the intermediate preferences of the other countries to bring free-riders into the fold of providing the public good.

These multilateral arrangements were uneasy but successful through the mid 1960s. The United States found some relief in its balance of payments deficits through the convertibility of European currencies and the already enormous supply of dollars circulating in the world markets. These Eurodollars and Eurocurrencies—national currencies circulating outside of their home countries—provided pools of liquidity that before were created only through the export of U.S. dollars. In 1968, the Group of Ten and the IMF created Special Drawing Rights (SDRs), the first international currency that could be used to assist countries with balance of payments problems.

By the early 1970s, however, U.S. preferences for providing monetary management shifted again. Benjamin Cohen (1977, 103–104) attributed this shift directly to the U.S. involvement in the Vietnam War.

> After 1965, however, the situation reversed itself, as a direct consequence of the escalation of hostilities in Vietnam. America's economy began to overheat, and inflation began to gain momentum. The Bretton Woods system was tailor-made to promote the transmission of this inflation abroad. With exchange rates pegged, tradable-goods price increases in the largest of all trading nations were immediately radiated outward to the rest of the world economy.

In 1970, the United States suffered its first trade deficit since before World War II due to the overvalued dollar abroad and inflation at home. These pressures caused the U.S. preferences for providing the public good of monetary management to shift from the privileged preference ordering to the intermediate preference ordering.

> The period of postwar recovery was over: Europe and Japan had become reinvigorated giants, not only willing but able to compete aggressively with America in markets at home and abroad. The cost of subordinating U.S. economic interests to the presumed political advantage of now strengthened allies was becoming ever more intolerable. (Cohen 1977, 102–103)

The problem of providing the public good of monetary stabilization had finally evolved into a Prisoner's Dilemma, as illustrated in figure 4.4.

Other Countries

United States	Do Not Contribute Good (D)	Contribute Good (C)
Do Not Contribute Good (D)	[2, 2]	4, 1 *
Contribute Good (C)	1, 4 *	3, 3 *

Figure 4.4. **Public Goods Game for Monetary Management—1971 and Beyond. United States: Intermediate Preferences; Others: Intermediate Preferences.** *Source:* author.

The interactive characteristics of the Prisoner's Dilemma are well known. Rapoport and Guyer (1966, 211) classify it as a game with a strongly stable deficient equilibrium, and it is the only game in that classification (#12). As noted earlier, the Prisoner's Dilemma is often equated with the public goods problem. Its logical outcome is for all players to free-ride, creating a deficient outcome when all players would benefit from mutual cooperation, yet there is no logic internal to the game that will provide that outcome. This is attractive to public goods theorists because it seems to replicate observed public good behavior, the public good is under supplied. Cooperation is possible, but only through manipulating conditions external to the game such as side payments, repeated play, or future discounting. These artifacts of cooperation have been the center of the neoliberal research program's "anarchy problematique."

The change in U.S. preferences was not merely a theoretical shift. The country acted on the new preferences in a most dramatic way when, on August 15, 1971, President Nixon announced in a nationally televised address that the United States would suspend the convertibility of the dollar to gold (Nixon 1971). This decision effectively marked the end of the Bretton Woods system. It would survive on paper until the Jamaica Conference in 1976 when the leading IMF members decided to legalize floating exchange rates, reduce the role of gold as a reserve value, increase IMF quotas, increase funds available for developing countries, and, most important, let each country determine its own par value (Gilpin 1987, 141).

The process of providing a global public good should not be viewed monolithically as a Prisoner's Dilemma that always devolves into mutual defection. The process can be much more nuanced. Global public goods are produced by those whose preferences for the goods are such that the benefits they receive from the goods exceed the costs of providing the good. They are willing to provide the good by themselves, if they must, in order to avoid losing the quantity of the good that they themselves would provide. The utility-based model of public goods presented in this chapter illustrated why the United States was willing to provide all (or most) of the cost of stabilizing the monetary system immediately after World War II. The model also illustrated that as the U.S. preferences for providing monetary stabilization shifted, the interactive dynamics between the United States and the rest of the countries in the system changed, leading to different behaviors by the players and ultimately to the United States stepping away from its identity as a monetary leader.

NOTES

1. The view that a single, economically powerful state must manage policies to stabilize the international monetary system lies at the heart of hegemonic stability theory in international relations, which will be discussed below. See Gilpin (2001, 100); Keohane (1980 and 1982); Krasner (1975); and Snidal (1985).

2. Richard Blackden (2011) reported that Bretton Woods, New Hampshire was chosen because John Maynard Keynes could not face a conference in the heat of Washington, DC in July.

3. The ten members were Belgium, Canada, France, Italy, Japan, the Netherlands, Sweden, the United Kingdom, the United States, and West Germany.

4. In figure 4.1, Nash equilibria are shown in **bold**, Rapoport & Guyer's (1966) Natural Outcome is in [brackets], and Pareto Optimal outcomes are noted with an asterisk (*). This format will be used for all subsequent games.

FIVE

Collective Security as a Global Public Good

IS MILITARY INTERVENTION A PUBLIC GOOD?

On March 24, 1999, the combined forces of the North Atlantic Treaty Organization (NATO) began an aerial bombing campaign against the state known then as the Federal Republic of Yugoslavia (FRY).[1] NATO's actions were taken to "prevent more human suffering and more repression and violence against the civilian population of Kosovo," and to "prevent instability spreading in the region" (NATO 1999b). Kosovo, a semi-autonomous region within the borders of the FRY populated by an ethnic Albanian Muslim majority, had been the site of increasingly violent ethnic tensions in the years prior to the NATO action. Diplomatic efforts on the part of the United Nations and individual nation-states did not prevent the FRY from engaging in widespread human rights abuses and alleged ethnic cleansing against the population of Kosovo. This led Javier Solana, secretary general of NATO, to conclude that "All efforts to achieve a negotiated, political solution to the Kosovo crisis having failed, no alternative is open but to take military action" (NATO 1999a). While there was significant controversy over NATO's military response, there was widespread support in the international community for some action against the FRY as evidenced by three prior UN Security Council resolutions calling for the FRY to cease its actions against the people of Kosovo. None of these resolutions directly authorized the use of force. Since decisions by the North Atlantic Council (the ruling body within NATO) are by consensus only, all nineteen NATO members agreed with or acquiesced with the decision to begin the military campaign. While many states denounced the use of force, NATO's actions to halt the human rights abuses, stop alleged ethnic cleansing, and stabilize the Balkan region, nevertheless provided a service to the interests of its members, its European neighbors, and, arguably, to the international community at large.

It may not be easy to see military intervention as a public good. Like the discussions about epidemics and financial instability in the last chapter, security problems can grow and engulf regions or the world in conflict. The assassination of Archduke Ferdinand in 1914 led to a conflict between Austria and Serbia that led to World War I. If a local conflict that can lead to regional or global conflict is a public bad, then is an attempt to prevent or end that conflict necessarily a public good? Military intervention to protect humanitarian rights or ensure collective security is a public good if it does not result in an asymmetric increase in power that accrues to the providers of the good that puts other states at risk and if the benefit to the whole community of states outweighs the collateral damage to some of the states. These are, of course, subjective criteria, over which there is likely to be substantial disagreement.

Military intervention is always about asymmetric distribution of power. At minimum, intervention attempts to deprive the party that is the target of the intervention of its power, or even its existence. Since states often exist in a network of alliances, alignments, or spheres of influence, interventions affect the power distributions of states beyond the target state as well. Interventions are meant to increase the security and power of the states that initiate the action. In this sense, they may be better analyzed as club goods than pure public goods. Club goods only provide benefits to those who are members of the club. The benefits of the good cannot be excluded from the members of the club and they are not used up in consumption. Krahmann (2008) claims that whether collective security is a public good or not depends on the reason for the security action. Collective security for prevention is typically a public good while collective security actions for deterrence are more likely to be club goods and efforts to survive a threat are becoming private goods with the privatization of security firms. Engerer (2011, 139) notes that security can take on the characteristics of all four types of goods. Security acts like a private good when commercial firms provide local protection. It acts like a club good when states enter a collective security agreement to address a purely regional problem. International security has the characteristics of a common pool resource when military assets are expended in one conflict, limiting their availability for other situations, and it can be characterized as a pure public good when a collective security arrangement brings stability to the world at large. Engerer concludes, however, that "With regard to national- and international-level security, this is still predominantly provided as a public good" (2011, 144). Olson and Zeckhauser (1966, 267) claimed that international organizations must serve a common interest of the member states and noted that NATO's common interest is protecting its members from a common enemy. "The analogy with a nation-state is obvious. Those goods and services, such as defense, that the government provides in the *common* interest of the citizenry, are usually called 'public goods'" (emphasis in the original). Olson and Zeckhauser (1966, 272) also note that "However important the non-collective benefits of alliances may be, there can be little doubt that above all, alliances produce public goods."

Was NATO's bombardment of the FRY in 1999 a global public good? For it to be a public good, it must first be a "good." That is, it must provide benefits rather than liabilities to a significant number of states. Outcry against NATO's actions taken without explicit United Nations Security Council authorization was loud and widespread. However, demands for the FRY to cease its actions against the people of Kosovo were virtually unanimous in the international community prior to the start of the bombing and many states that called for the aerial campaign to stop continued to demand that FRY withdraw from Kosovo.[2] There was broad agreement with the common interest of stopping the FRY but significant disagreement about the means used by NATO. Does a product or service have to be universally desired to be a public good? No, a public park that serves the needs of a broad community may be opposed by its neighbors that do not want outsiders coming into their neighborhood. To be a public good, the product or service must be desired by a significant number of states and its benefits, or liabilities, cannot be excluded and cannot be consumed in usage. To be a global public good its effects must be felt worldwide and across time. NATO's aerial bombardment of the FRY in 1999 met these criteria.

This chapter examines NATO's aerial bombardment of FRY in 1999 as a global public good. As with any public good, the primary question is why did some agents provide the good while others did not? Non-excludability ensured that they would receive the benefits of the good whether or not they participated in the provision of the good. The agents in this situation were the member states of NATO and, to a lesser extent, other states in the region.

NATO'S AERIAL BOMBARDMENT OF THE FEDERAL REPUBLIC OF YUGOSLAVIA IN 1999

Tensions between the ethnically Albanian Muslim population of Kosovo, known as Kosovars, and their Orthodox Christian Serbian neighbors can be traced back for centuries. These tensions were renewed with the breakup of Yugoslavia in the early 1990s. President Slobodan Milosevic changed Yugoslavia's constitution in 1989 to reduce the autonomy that the province of Kosovo enjoyed since 1974 and he used Serbian nationalism within the province to bolster his support in a crumbling Yugoslavia. In response, Kosovar nationalists formed the Kosovo Liberation Army (KLA) in 1996 and began to attack Serbian targets. Serbian authorities responded with increased repression and ethnic attacks. Between March

5 and 7, 1998, Serb security forces killed fifty Kosovars in the village of Prekaz, prompting the United States Secretary of State Madeline Albright, to declare that "We are not going to stand by and watch the Serbian authorities do in Kosovo what they can no longer get away with doing in Bosnia" (Erlanger 1998).

A group of major powers known as the "Contact Group" met in London on March 9 to discuss the rising violence in Kosovo while U.S. diplomat Robert Gelbard met with Milosevic in Belgrade.[3] The Contact Group recommended that the UN Security Council pass a resolution imposing an arms embargo on FRY and demanding that FRY cease attacks on the population of Kosovo. The Security Council passed Resolution 1160 in response to the Contact Group's request, with all members voting in favor except China, that abstained. This was the first of three UN Security Council Resolutions (1160, 1203, and 1239) passed in 1998 that demanded that Serbia halt its ethnic violence against the Kosovars. The Russian Federation, as a member of the Contact Group, supported the first two resolutions but abstained from the last one. Russia refused to allow more strident language to be included in any of the resolutions that would have authorized the use of force, under threat of veto. It was Russia's refusal to consider the use of force along with Milosevic's clear rejection of all diplomatic efforts to end the crisis that prompted NATO to threaten to use military force. NATO had once before used aerial bombardment to stop FRY and Croatian aggression against Bosnia in 1994.

On June 11, U.S. Secretary of Defense William Cohen urged NATO ministers to begin planning a military intervention and NATO began military exercises in the region to signal their willingness to act (WGBH 2014). On September 24, the North Atlantic Council of NATO issued an "ACTWARN," a decision that asked member states to identify assets needed to conduct an aerial campaign against FRY (NATO 1998a). The crisis came to a head in early 1999 when FRY forces attacked the village of Račak killing forty-five Kosovars. Milosevic refused to let international investigators enter the area and claimed the massacre was the work of the KLA. On January 30, 1999, NATO issued a force activation order to its members and, in a press release referring to the Račak massacre, stated that "It stands ready to act and rules out no option to ensure full respect by both sides in Kosovo for the requirements of the international community" (NATO 1999a).

On February 6, representatives of Kosovo, FRY, the European Union, and the Contact Group met in Rambouillet, France in one last diplomatic effort to resolve the crisis. Negotiations continued until February 23 when an Interim Agreement was issued that ensured Kosovo's right to democratic self-determination and that the KLA would disarm and FRY forces in Kosovo would be reduced to fifteen hundred (Krieger 2001b).

The Rambouillet meeting ended without the parties endorsing the agreement. Commanders of the KLA announced on March 8 that they would support the agreement but on March 12, Milosevic rejected it out of hand (Kritsiotis 2000, 339).

On March 24, NATO began its aerial bombardment campaign. Sixteen of the nineteen NATO members participated in the campaign in some way with combat missions flown by eleven member states.[4] The aerial campaign lasted for seventy-eight days. NATO's initial strategy was to hit high value military targets. Most of these targets were destroyed in the first few days of the campaign so NATO turned to official and economic targets, including government buildings, bridges, infrastructure, and some factories. Although NATO claimed to minimize civilian losses, many civilian assets were destroyed by mistake or collateral damage including the Chinese Embassy in Belgrade, where three Chinese civilians were killed and twenty were injured. The bombing campaign continued until June 10 when NATO ceased the operation after FRY troops began withdrawing from Kosovo under a Military Technical Agreement and settlement brokered, in part, by the Russian Federation.

NATO'S IDENTITIES, PREFERENCES, AND INTERACTIONS

This section examines the identities and preferences of the United States. Canada, and Greece during the NATO operation. Although "coalition of the willing" was used to describe the collection of states that participated in 2003 invasion of Iraq, this label might be better applied to the members of NATO involved with the Kosovo campaign. Decision making in the North Atlantic Council is by consensus. Therefore, all nineteen members had to agree that NATO should engage the aerial bombing campaign. Yet, not all members contributed to the public good and, among those that did, not all members contributed equally.

The United States has long held the identity as a leader within NATO. It is the most powerful member and is often the most vocal. In 1999, the United States provided 55 percent of the total military expenditures of all NATO members and 32.5 percent of all NATO member armed forces personnel. The next largest contributors of NATO expenditures in 1999 were Germany at 10.5 percent and France at 10.2 percent (NATO 2000a).

NATO's aerial bombing of the FRY occurred against the backdrop of the changing international system. The Soviet Union disbanded only seven years before the beginning of the campaign. NATO spent those seven years in serious introspection about the role of the Atlantic alliance in a post–Cold War world. Members of the Clinton and George H. W. Bush administration and many scholars thought that U.S. leadership in this time of transition was critical for the stability and security in Europe. Robert Art, an international relations scholar, stated that

> America's military presence helps maintain the benign security environment within Western Europe. America's balancing role is a principal instrument that helps keep both external threats and internal fears from corroding Western Europe's cohesion . . . The American presence can both assist the movement towards greater union and also prevent corrosive nationalistic backsliding.
>
> By its absence or presence, therefore, the United States will influence what Western Europe looks like at the end of the Maastricht process, and therefore what the rest of Europe will look like. In the engagement view, the United States must be present, not absent. (Art 1996, 38–39)

Richard Holbrooke, the assistant secretary of state for European and Eurasian affairs in the Clinton administration, echoed these views.

> Today an equally prosperous Western Europe (and Japan, which has a stake in and benefits from a stable Europe) will have to put up the bulk of the actual financial assistance, but the United States must continue to play a leading part. In the words of Secretary of State Warren Christopher, the central goal of the United States is "to help extend to all of Europe the benefits and obligations of the same liberal trading and collective security order that have been pillars of strength for the West." (Holbrooke 1995, 40)

President Clinton clearly defined the United States identity with respect to NATO in a speech in Detroit in 1996, where he stated:

> America truly is *the world's indispensable nation*. There are times when only America can make the difference between war and peace, between freedom and repression, between hope and fear. We cannot and should not try to be the world's policeman. But where our interests and values are clearly at stake, and where we can make a difference, we must act and lead . . . The United States will continue to take the lead in NATO, especially in the southern region where the most immediate threats to peace exist. But we welcome our allies' willingness to shoulder a greater share of the burden and to assume greater leadership. (Clinton 1996; emphasis added)

A nation-state's identity is born of internal and external structures (Wendt 1999, 224). The perceptions and preferences of the state's leaders are important in this process, but so are the perceptions and preferences of the state's people. Forty-three percent of the American public supported possible U.S. participation in a NATO campaign one month prior to the beginning of the bombing. Three weeks after the NATO action began, 61 percent of the public supported it and 52 percent of the public supported using American ground troops. Among those that supported using ground troops, two-thirds believed that the United States had a moral obligation to help refugees from Kosovo. President Clinton maintained high approval ratings (60 percent) throughout the NATO action (Gillespie 1999).

The United States' identity as the "indispensable nation" accompanied by domestic support for action against the FRY defined American preferences in the Kosovo situation. U.S. intentions were clearly stated in a number of different international forums. It was the United States that initially recommended that NATO prepare for an aerial campaign against the FRY. In December, 1992, President George W. Bush issued a "Christmas Warning" to Slobodan Milosevic that indicated that the United States would be willing to use force unilaterally to halt FRY human rights abuses in Kosovo. This warning was repeated by the Clinton administration (WGBH 2014). Given its willingness to act alone, American preferences for the public good of collective military action against the FRY in Kosovo aligned with the special preference ordering illustrated in figure 3.2, where the agent is willing to provide the public good by itself, rather than forego the quantity of public good that it can provide.

Since a player with the special preference ordering would prefer to contribute the public good on its own over no good being produced, there is no reason to model America's strategic interaction with the rest of NATO. The nature of the Kosovo campaign does, however, raise an interesting problem for the U.S. decision to participate in the bombardment of the FRY. The campaign would only be successful if NATO committed to a significant, or perhaps excessive, level of bombardment. The NATO aerial bombardment of FRY targets during the Kosovo conflict was a threshold public good. A threshold good is a good "where the benefits of the [good] are only experienced once the cumulative quantity of the good surpasses a certain level" (Sandler 2006, 10). If the threshold is beyond what can be afforded by the special privileged player, then sole provision of the good will not succeed and the player must rely on cooperation with others to produce the good. If the threshold is beyond the combined effort of the collective, then the good is unobtainable.

Critics of the attack believed that the threshold could not be reached with air power alone. Senator John McCain, a U.S. Navy fighter pilot during the Vietnam War, stated in a *New York Times* article on the morning following the beginning of the war that, "These bombs are not going to do the job. You're just going to solidify the determination of the Serbs to resist a peace agreement. You'd have to drop the bridges and turn off the lights in Belgrade to have even a remote chance of changing Milosevic's mind" (Apple 1999). David Owen, the former British foreign secretary, concurred. "The only thing that will get Milosevic's attention is the real prospect that you're going to sweep his troops out of Kosovo

74 Chapter Five

and stay there to keep them out" (Apple 1999). The article continued with the speculation that a successful effort to remove Serbian forces from Kosovo would require more than one hundred thousand ground troops. Although the NATO campaign did not use ground troops, Senator McCain's prediction eventually proved to be correct. The aerial bombardment lasted for seventy-eight days. NATO flew 10,484 strike sorties and dropped approximately twenty-eight thousand bombs and other munitions. All the bridges across the Danube in the FRY were destroyed and the electrical grid in Serbia's three largest cities was attacked during the first three days of the campaign, leaving 80 percent of Serbia without power (Lambeth 2001, location 1083).

Figure 5.1 models the U.S. decision to provide the public good. This is merely a logical model of the decision and does not represent the quantities involved in the decision. The vertical line at B represents the amount of the public good that the United States believes will be supplied by the rest of NATO. The combined forces of the United States (Air Force and Navy) flew approximately 80 percent of all strike sorties during the war. The other NATO members delivered only 4,703 (17 percent) of the 28,018 munitions expended during the campaign (Lambeth 2001, location 1400). Points CC_1 and CD_1 represent optimum levels for the United States of cooperative provision of the good and sole provision of the good respectively, if there was no threshold point. These quantities of the good are unobtainable because neither of them meets the threshold level represented by the line TT. NATO initially expected that the entire aerial campaign could be completed with two to three days of bombing directed at approximately fifty targets (Lambeth 2001, location 4218). NATO command realized that these numbers were inadequate as soon as the campaign began, but they were able to identify only one hundred targets that met the rules of engagement by the end of the first week of the campaign. U.S. Army General Wesley Clark, the supreme allied commander in Europe (SACEUR) went to the North Atlantic Council of NATO to get approval to expand the target list to include a broad range of military assets. His staff generated a list of approximately two thousand targets, some of which had questionable military significance. This decision is represented on the model in figure 5.1 by moving from point CC_1 to point CC_2. The move achieves the threshold level at TT but places the United States on a lower utility curve where the costs in personnel, dollars, and materiel of reaching the threshold exceeded what the United States expected or wanted to pay.

Any group with at least one member with a privileged or special privileged preference ordering for the public good will succeed in providing the public good. Members with special privileged preferences actually prefer providing the goods by themselves over free-riding because they do not want to lose the quantity of he good they can provide by them-

Private Good (Y)

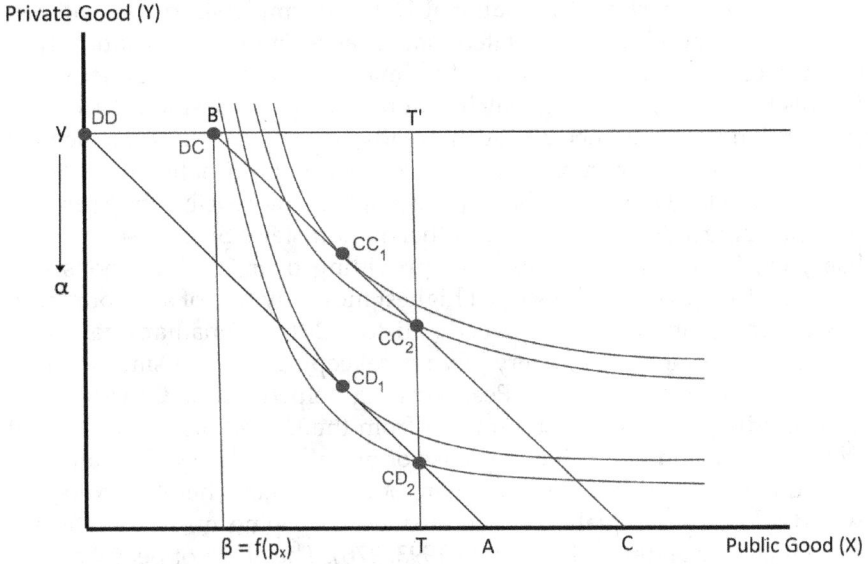

Figure 5.1.   U.S. decision to participate in the Kosovo campaign as a threshold good.
Source: author.

selves. Members with the privileged preference ordering would prefer to free-ride but will provide the good by themselves, if necessary. The member-states of NATO, as a collective, can be modeled with a privileged preference ordering for the aerial campaign against the FRY (see figure 3.3). This is confirmed first by the unanimous vote on January 30, 1999 by the North Atlantic Council to empower the NATO secretary general to authorized air strikes against the FRY. Even Greece, that later refused to participate in the campaign, voted in favor of the air strikes. NATO's collective preferences for the campaign are also confirmed by the widespread support for the actions among the member states' citizens. In a poll conducted within two weeks of the beginning of the campaign among eleven NATO member-states and five other nation-states, well over half the populations of the member-states supported the campaign except for Italy and the three states admitted to membership in 1999 (Czech Republic, Hungary, and Poland). Support varied among the six non-member states polled from a high in Croatia (82 percent), which had its own ethnic conflict with the FRY, to a low in Russia (just 2 percent), which officially opposed the campaign in the United Nations Security Council (Everts 2003).[5]

Canada's identity in international relations is very much tied up with its role in peacekeeping operations. General Paul D. Mason, chief of staff of Canada's Department of National Defense, emphasized this national identity in a speech when he stated that "Peacekeeping comes naturally to Canadians, as history has shown. The image of a Canadian soldier wearing his blue beret, standing watch at some lonely outpost in a strife-torn foreign land with binoculars at the ready, is very much an element of the modern Canadian mosaic, and a proud part of our national heritage" (Mason 1988, 41). Canada has participated in more UN observer and peacekeeping missions than any other nation-state. Since 1947 Canada has participated in sixty missions, providing over 120,000 troops and personnel. Canada has the second highest mortality rate of any country in UN peacekeeping missions (Canada History 2013). Canadians have participated in some way in every UN peacekeeping mission since the first mission in Palestine in 1948. Peacekeeping helped define Canada's role as a middle power and distinguish it from the United States in the Cold War struggle and even give it a sense of moral superiority. This allowed Canadians to identify as "middlemen, honest brokers, helpful fixers in a world where these qualities were rare. Peacekeeping made us different and somehow better" (Granatstein 1993, 276). The effect of peacekeeping in the Canadian national identity is captured passionately by Sean Maloney (2005, 41).

> Why, exactly, are these distinctions important? Are not all Canadian military personnel "peacekeepers"? Has UN peacekeeping not been the stock in trade for Canadian soldiers since Lester B. Pearson invented peacekeeping in 1956 during the Suez Crisis? Isn't our national identity based on the fact that we do peacekeeping while others fight wars? Are we not morally superior because Canada engages in peacekeeping?

Eric Wagner argued that Canada's altruistic motivations in international relations really formed a "myth of peacekeeping" that supported its true strategic interests of preventing local conflicts from escalating to nuclear war in the Cold War competition between the East and the West. As such, Canada's peacekeeping efforts were seldom non-partisan in this struggle and worked to maintain a pro-Western status quo (Wagner 2006). The myth was further exposed when evidence of human rights abuses committed by Canadian peacekeepers in Somalia, Haiti, and elsewhere came to light (Whitworth 2005).

Canada was fully committed to the NATO aerial campaign—perhaps even more so than the United States. At the beginning of the campaign, when the United States was reluctant even to discuss anything more than air strikes, the Canadian government spoke openly of expanding the war to include ground troops and stated that Canadian soldiers would participate in a ground operation (Sallot 1999, A16). Robert Fowler, Canada's permanent representative to the United Nations in 1999, clearly stated Canada's commitment to the campaign in the UN Security Council debate on March 24, 1999.

> The continuing oppression in Kosovo by the Government in Belgrade, through its armed forces and police; the continuing failure on the part of the Milosevic Government to implement the agreements it has made with the OSCE and NATO; and its continuing refusal to act in compliance with the requirements of successive Security Council resolutions—actions which, I repeat, have only contributed to an increase in tension and have created a major humanitarian disaster—have left NATO with no choice but to take action. (UN Security Council 1999, 5)

Canada's identity and interests generated the privileged preference ordering for the public good of collective military campaign against the FRY that is shown in figure 3.3. It clearly preferred participation in the campaign over not participating but was unwilling and unable to provide the threshold of the good by itself. Canada's choice to participate in the provision of the good of the military intervention was easy in the strategic interaction between Canada and the other NATO member-states as illustrated in figure 5.2.

The Rest of the NATO Collective

Canada	Do Not Contribute Good (D)	Contribute Good (C)
Do Not Contribute Good (D)	1, 1	3, 2
Contribute Good (C)	2, 3	[4, 4] *

Figure 5.2. Canada's decision to contribute to the Kosovo campaign. *Source*: author.

The game in figure 5.2 is a No Conflict Game (Rapoport and Guyer 1966). Each player has a dominant strategy to contribute to the NATO campaign and the outcome provides both players with their best payoff. The outcome is a unique Nash equilibrium and corresponds to the Rapoport and Guyer natural outcome of the game.

Canada's participation in the Kosovo campaign was second in scale only to the United States. Canada supplied eighteen CF-18 fighter bombers for the operation and was responsible for 10 percent of the ordinance dropped on FRY targets during the bombardment (Haglund and Sens 2000, 195; Manolache and Chis 2015). Canadian pilots flew 678 combat sorties and dropped 532 bombs—nearly five hundred thousand pounds of explosives (Bashow et al. 2000, 55).

Greece was the only member of NATO that refused to participate in the Kosovo campaign. Before Macedonia declared its independence in 1991, Greece shared a border with Yugoslavia. A poll conducted in Greece during the conflict found that 99.5 percent of the respondents opposed the war. Just under 85 percent thought the war was just a NATO "show of force," and only 2.5 percent believed the war was fought to end ethnic cleansing (*Irish Times* 1999, 13). Greece was struggling with an identity crisis. International social pressures identified Greece as a member of NATO and a supporter of its collective security arrangements. Regional social pressures pushed for an identity in solidarity with its Balkan neighbor against external influence. Domestic social pressures on the government, facing a highly contested national election in June, pushed its identity to remain independent from American influence with nearly unanimous public opinion against the war. The depth of this identity crisis was highlighted in a speech given by Costas Simitis, the Greek prime minister, in April 1999.

> We work for the rapprochement of the Balkan states with the European Union and we contribute decisively to the inter-Balkan cooperation at a multilateral and a bilateral level . . . It is in this light that we see our role in the current crisis in Kosovo. In front of our eyes is unfolding a humanitarian tragedy of proportions unseen in Europe since the Second World War . . . As members of NATO we have actively cooperated with our allies on this issue. We have however stated from the beginning that we will not participate in military operations. We are neighbors with Yugoslavia and we would like a political solution. Yugoslavia should give the people of Kosovo a wide measure of autonomy, respect their human rights and seek a peaceful solution to the problem. We have unequivocally condemned the practice of "ethnic cleansing" that Serbia has pursued. (Krieger 2001a, 404–405)

This identity crisis was fed by the desire to lead a Balkan-wide foreign policy; pride in its identity as a member of the European society of states;

concerns about Turkey's geopolitical intentions in the peninsula; substantial mistrust of American motives; and widespread anti-Americanism among the Greek population.

George Papandreou, the minister of foreign affairs of Greece at the time of the Kosovo campaign and, later, the prime minister of Greece, noted that Greece has a dual identity tied both to the institutions of Western Europe and to the Balkans. "As the only full member of the European Union (EU) and NATO in the region, we feel a responsibility to represent the interests of our neighbors in these institutions and to help them prepare for integration into the European framework" (Papandreou 2000, 75). Papandreou claimed that Greece created a regional strategy he called "a total Balkan approach" that was "founded upon the principles of respect for sovereignty and territorial integrity, respect of existing borders, and dissuasion of separatist tendencies and divisive ideologies" (Papandreou 2000, 76).

The break-up of the former Yugoslavia created tensions for Greece, especially when Macedonia declared independence in 1991. Disputes over the name of the country, fears of Macedonian irredentism, and conflicting claims about Macedonian cultural heritage continue to this day (BBC 2018). Turkey's early recognition of Macedonian independence along with its improving relations with other Balkan states after the fall of Yugoslavia concerned Greece greatly and renewed its fears of Turkish influence in the peninsula (Larrabee 2005, 417). In a region where religion determines political alignment, orthodox Greece saw a natural ally with orthodox Serbia, both bordered by newly emergent Muslim countries.

Greece struggled to improve relations with the rest of the Balkan countries throughout the 1990s, but the relationships remained fragile as NATO's Kosovo campaign unfolded (Larrabee 2005). The campaign presented a direct challenge to Greece's attempt to establish leadership in the Balkans. Greece had to balance its interests in maintaining good relations with NATO and Western Europe while not alienating its Balkan ally, Serbia. Prime Minister Simitis spoke on national television on April 5, 1999, stating,

> In order to deal with the dangers in the region, we must cooperate with the countries of the European Union, and safeguard our role in NATO . . . The worst we could do would be to marginalize the country through heated reactions. In this case, Greece would become part of the Balkan problem and not a part of its solution. (Associated Press 1999)

Greece was particularly concerned with maintaining its relationship with Western Europe since a decision on its application for entry to the European Monetary Union was due in fall, 1999. Greek officials were also concerned about how the United States reacted to its refusal to participate in NATO's aerial campaign. Greece needed future U.S. support in its on-going disputes with Turkey over Cyprus and territorial disputes in the Aegean Sea (Migdalovitz 1999).

While Greek leaders tried to maintain good relations with their NATO allies, the Greek populace pressured them to condemn NATO's actions. Greece's sympathy for Serbia was driven by popular support rooted in cultural and religious identification with its Balkan neighbor and fueled by a deep anti-American sentiment (See Michas 2002, 5 and Larrabee 2005, 410). Anti-American sentiment in modern Greece began after World War II with the implementation of the Truman Doctrine and the Marshall Plan. Anti-Americanism emerged as a reaction to the official anti-communist ideology of the Greek government that aligned with those institutions and ultimately created a cross-party convergence of opposition to American influence in Greek affairs (Lialiouti 2015, 43). Anti-Americanism was exacerbated by frustration with the failure of the United States to support Greece's interests in the conflict with Great Britain and later with Turkey over Cyprus. Public opposition to the NATO campaign was due less to pro-Serbian and pro-orthodox sentiments and more to anti-Americanism and a leftist tradition in the Greek political culture (Lialiouti 2011, 127). This anti-Americanism was manifested in a poll conducted in Greece during the Kosovo campaign where 69.7 percent of the respondents felt that U.S. President Clinton should be tried for war crimes (*Irish Times* 1999). Anti-Americanism was further stirred up during the Kosovo campaign by Greek news media that reported that the real reason for bombing the FRY was to promote American geopolitical interests in the Balkan peninsula (Kondopoulou 2002).

Keith Brown and Dimitri Theodossopoulos confirmed the effect of the general anti-American sentiment and the Greek news accounts of the Kosovo bombing through a series of ethnographic interviews with residents of Patras, a town in southwest Greece in late spring 1999. The responses of the subjects of the study were universally opposed to the NATO campaign. A number of anecdotal rumors emerged as explanations for NATO's actions. Among these were the belief that the Americans needed to use up arms that were approaching their use-by dates and the assertion that President Clinton staged the NATO bombing to divert attention away from his domestic problems stemming from the Monica Lewinsky affair (Brown and Theodossopoulos 2003, 324–325).

Greece's complex identity certainly did not lead it to the same privileged preference ordering for the public good of the aerial campaign that other states in NATO held. While Greece saw virtue in the campaign stemming both from the cessation of human rights abuses in Kosovo and from its continued support of the Atlantic alliance, the benefits did not warrant any real participation in the provision of the public good. Its identity created interests that led to the latent preference ordering illustrated in figure 3.5, where the individual desires to consume the benefit of the public good but has no incentive to provide any quantity of the good —either by itself or in cooperation with the rest of the collective.[6]

If Greece perceived the rest of NATO to have the privileged preference ordering, as discussed above, Greece's decision to contribute to the NATO campaign is modeled in the game in figure 5.3.

Both players have dominant strategies in the game in figure 5.3. Greece's dominant strategy is not to contribute to the NATO campaign while the rest of NATO's dominant strategy is to contribute. The outcome (DC = 4,2) is the unique Nash equilibrium and is also the Rapoport and Guyer natural outcome. There was little that the rest of NATO members could do to encourage Greece's contribution. The game is not threat vulnerable. That is, if NATO threatened not to pursue the aerial campaign, Greece would not change its decision.

The Rest of the NATO Collective

Greece	Do Not Contribute Good (D)	Contribute Good (C)
Do Not Contribute Good (D)	3, 1	[4, 2]*
Contribute Good (C)	1, 3*	2, 4*

Figure 5.3.   Greece's decision not to contribute to the Kosovo campaign. *Source*: author.

CONCLUSIONS—INDIVIDUAL DECISIONS
IN COLLECTIVE SECURITY

Olson and Zeckhauser's article on the economic theory of alliances (1966) set the tone for much of the scholarship on military alliances and public goods that followed. Their questions were simple. How do alliances share the burdens of collective security if alliances are pure public goods? Their answer, known as the exploitation hypothesis, was that a since a state's gross national product (GNP) is a good measure of the benefit derived from collective security, states are willing to contribute to the cost of the alliance proportional to their GNP.[7] This means that larger states contribute more than smaller states. Since the benefits of a pure public good are non-excludable, smaller states are likely to exploit this correlation between national income and contribution by free-riding on the expected contribution of the larger states. Published in the middle of the Cold War, Olson and Zeckhauser's theory and data focused on the contributions of NATO members. Oneal (1990, 281) claimed that the ability of national income to explain contributions to the alliance decreased over time and noted that Sandler and Forbes (1980) showed that although the correlation between GDP and alliance contribution remained in the right direction, the relationship was not statistically significant after 1966. Scholars scrambled to explain this phenomenon.[8] One approach was to note that as NATO shifted its primary Cold War role from strategic nuclear deterrence against a Soviet attack to defending Western Europe against a Soviet invasion, the nature of the alliance shifted away from being a pure public good to being a common pool resource (Sandler and Cauley 1975). Their reasoning was that the flexible response strategy adopted by NATO in December, 1967, meant that military resources in a crisis might be expended in one battle leaving fewer resources to use in another battle. The benefits of defense would still be non-excludable, but the military resources could now be used up meaning that they are now rival in consumption.

All of this scholarship is a worthy effort to understand NATO burden-sharing during the Cold War, but the Atlantic alliance's mission, indeed its raison d'être, changed in 1991 with the fall of the Soviet Union. Not once during the Cold War did NATO deploy military assets in a direct combat mission. All of the discussion of burden-sharing during the Cold War related to the member-states sharing the burden of *preparing* for conflict. NATO's first military deployment was operation Anchor Guard in August, 1990, in which NATO early warning aircraft were deployed to Turkey to protect against Iraqi air attack during the first Gulf War. NATO's first combat mission was Operation Deny Flight in 1993, which started as the enforcement of a no-fly zone over Bosnia-Herzegovina and resulted in NATO's first combat engagement in an air battle over Banja Luka in 1994 (NATO 2017). NATO's first large scale combat operation was Operation Deliberate Force in August and September of 1995. This operation targeted Bosnian Serb forces to stop massive human rights abuses during the Bosnian Civil War. With these operations, NATO moved from the deterrent and defensive use of force during the Cold War to the compellent use of force that has characterized its missions in the Balkan peninsula, Libya, and Afghanistan in the post-Cold War world. Robert Art describes the compellent use of force as "the deployment of military power so as to be able either to stop an adversary from doing something that he has already undertaken or to get him to do something that he has not yet undertaken" (Art 1980, 7). Deterrent and defensive use of force, as practiced by NATO during the Cold War, are essentially passive activities. As Art points out, "The purpose of both is dissuasion—persuading others not to undertake actions harmful to oneself . . . Defense dissuades by presenting an unvanquishable military force. Deterrence dissuades by presenting the certainty of retaliatory devastation" (Art 1980, 7).

All three of these uses of force can be modeled as threshold goods. The difference between them lies in the level of uncertainty of the threshold. As Art notes, "The success of a deterrent threat is measured by its not having to be used" (Art 1980, 8). It is difficult to prove a negative. A state never knows if the threshold for deterrence has been reached since the attack may still be pending. The state only knows that the threshold was not reached when an attack occurs. Perhaps this explains why the two superpowers engaged in overkill arms races during the Cold War. The success of defensive use of force is the ability to withstand an attack. Unless the scale of the attack is overwhelming, as in the Blitzkrieg against Poland in 1939, there may be time to ramp resources up to the threshold as the attack continues. The level of a defensive threshold is unknown but it must be achieved quickly to avert disaster. The success of the compellent use of force is the ability to change the behavior of the target state. Compellent use of force includes non-military actions such as economic sanctions. The threshold necessary for compellent use of force is often reached in stages starting with low level diplomatic or economic activities and possibly ending in military action. In the case of the NATO campaign in Kosovo, NATO realized within a week of the start of the campaign that its level of effort would not be sufficient to compel the FRY to cease its actions against the Kosovars. General Wesley Clark quickly obtained permission from the Atlantic Council to change the targeting strategy and began to initiate massive sorties against diverse targets.

Threshold goods have a higher likelihood of being successfully supplied than many other types of public goods (Sandler 2004, 68). If the threshold is high, the members of the collective recognize that cooperative provision of the good increases the chance that the threshold will be met. Iceland and Luxembourg provided no support to the Kosovo campaign because they have no significant standing military. The Czech Republic, Hungary, and Poland provided no material support because they joined NATO only twelve days before the beginning of the campaign (NATO 1999c). NATO command did consider using air bases in the Czech Republic and Hungary. Greece refused to participate in the air war. All other NATO member provided some level of support for the operation. Combat missions were flown by Belgium, Canada, Denmark, France, Germany, Italy, the Netherlands, Norway, Spain, Turkey, the United Kingdom, and the United States (Lambeth 2001, locations 7770–778). Additional combat aircraft were provided by Portugal (Radio Renascenca 1999).

The utility-based model presented here did not attempt to explain whether or not NATO provided an optimal level of the public good. It did provide insight into individual states' decisions to participate in the campaign. Those decisions were driven by the states' preferences that reflected the identities that the states assumed. The United States played a leadership role, both in terms of its ability to provide material support for the campaign and in terms of its interests in achieving the outcomes. Its special privileged preference ordering led it to provide the greatest level of military support. Canada assumed its identity as a middle power peacekeeper and provided substantial support for the campaign. Greece, caught in a multi-dimensional struggle to define its identity, provided no assistance to the effort beyond its initial vote of approval. In each of these cases, the identities of the states determined the preferences that were the basis for their decisions to provide, or not provide, the good.

NOTES

1. The Federal Republic of Yugoslavia was formed in 1992 as a union of Serbia and Montenegro after the secession of Bosnia, Croatia, Macedonia, and Slovenia from Yugoslavia. Montenegro seceded from the union in 2006 and the region of Serbia changed its name to the Republic of Serbia, as it is known today (CIA 2017).

2. See Krieger (2001a, chapter 7) for a sampling of official reactions for and against the NATO campaign.

3. The Contact Group consisted of France, Germany, Italy, Russia, the United Kingdom, and the United States.

4. All of the NATO members contributed in some way to the campaign except Iceland and Luxembourg, that had no significant military assets to contribute, and Greece. Although Greece agreed to NATO's action in the North Atlantic Council, it could not generate domestic support to contribute to the campaign. Combat missions were flown by Belgium, Canada, Denmark, France, Germany, Italy,

Netherlands, Spain, Turkey, the United Kingdom, and the United States (Mano-lache and Chis 2015; and Lambeth 2001).

5. The data were drawn from a poll conducted by Angus Reid for *The Economist* except for the data for Netherlands, which were taken from a poll conducted by *TNS-Nipo* (Everts 2003). The NATO states included in the poll were Canada, the Czech Republic, Denmark, France, Germany, Hungary, Italy, Netherlands, Norway, Poland, United Kingdom, and the United States. The non-NATO states included in the poll were Croatia, Finland, Russia, Slovakia, and Ukraine.

6. There is no indication that Greece's preferences for the pubic good aligned with the intermediate preference ordering where the individual gains enough benefit from the good that it prefers collective provision of the good over no good being provided. While Greece apparently recognized some benefits of the aerial campaign, at no time did it indicate any willingness to participate in the military action.

7. Contributions to NATO are measured in military expenditures either as total expenditures or as a proportion of the state's gross domestic product.

8. See Sandler (1993) for an excellent review and critique of the scholarship that supported, critiqued, or extended Olson and Zechauser's original work.

Six

The Individual Decision to Provide Collective Security

Romania and the Kosovo Campaign

ROMANIAN IDENTITY AND YUGOSLAVIA FROM 1853 TO 1990

The Romanian national identity developed in four phases from the middle of the nineteenth century to the end of the twentieth century. The first phase from 1853 to 1919 marked the emergence of a unique Romanian identity with the formation of the modern Romanian state. The second phase occurred with the evolution of the Romanian identity in the interwar period as Romania struggled to maintain its independence and territorial integrity in the face of an increasingly hostile environment in Southern Europe. The third phase encompassed the redevelopment of Romanian identity in the communist period of the Cold War from 1945 to 1990. The next section of this chapter examines the shifting Romanian identity after the Cold War. Each of these phases is examined in light of the effect that identity formation and change had on interests and preferences in the relationship between Romania and Yugoslavia.

The earliest written reference to the peoples that populated present day Romania is found in a text by Herodotus in 514 B.C. (Malita 1970). Known as the Dacians, these people developed political structures as early as the third century B.C. and carried on diplomatic and trade relations with the Macedonians and later the Roman Empire. The Roman emperor Trajan succeeded in subduing the provinces of Banat and Walachia and parts of Transylvania in A.D. 101 to 106. This area became the northeast border of the Roman Empire and was flooded with colonists from around the empire (Keefe et al., 1972). Romania's Roman legacy has been a source of pride and identity that it has maintained to this day and that is reflected in its name. Romania was subject to successive barbaric invasions after the fall of the Roman Empire. The provinces maintained semi-autonomous rule as small principalities until the Ottoman invasions in the fifteenth century.

A unified Romanian identity began to emerge in the events that surrounded the Crimean War. In 1853, Russia demanded the right to protect orthodox Christian peoples throughout the Ottoman Empire. The Ottoman Porte refused this request and was backed by Great Britain and France that believed that the Russian request was an attempt by Russia to control the Ottoman Empire and subvert the balance of power in the eastern Mediterranean (Boia 1993, 6). Russia invaded Moldova and Walachia to threaten the Ottoman Empire. Great Britain and France declared war on Russia. The war was concluded during the Crimean campaign in 1856 with Russia's defeat. The Romanian provinces were put under a joint guarantee of European powers at the conclusion of the war, although they were still under Ottoman suzerainty (Boia 1993, 6–7). Elections were held under the supervision of the guaranteeing powers and both provinces elected Alexandru Ioan Cuza as their prince. This foreshadowed a process of Romanian unification and independence that would last from 1858 to 1877. Meanwhile, the Serbian state, which was also under Ottoman suzerainty, watched the events in the Romanian provinces closely and was the first state to recognize the dual princedom of Cuza formally. Serbia saw its hopes for its own independence from the Ottomans closely linked to the successful unification and independence of Romania.

Cuza's goal was twofold. Internally he had to build a Romanian unified identity and externally he had to gain recognition of that identity, constrained though it was by the Ottomans. France and Prussia were willing to identify a semi-autonomous unified Romania for such an entity could stand in opposition to Austrian interests in the region and to the Ottoman Empire. Russia was less willing to recognize the dual election, due in part to their loss of the protectorate over the two provinces. Russia came around to recognition once France had recognized the election to keep the Ottomans at bay. Ever the cautious balancer, Great Britain was reluctant to recognize the election until it was certified by the Porte. The Romanians, meanwhile, were hard at work identifying themselves as a key strategic player in the interplay of great power politics in the Balkan peninsula. "Moreover, the Romanians, perceiving that their greatest chance for success lay in demonstrating how Romanian union fitted in with the strategic considerations of those whom they sought to woo, never ceased to hammer away on this theme" (Bobango 1979, 82). The newly emerging Romanian identity was prescribing rules of behavior that served to define and constrain Romanian actions. Recognition of the dual election was finally received from all of the great powers in 1859.

Cuza faced an equally difficult task in creating a unified identity inside Romania. There were more than eighty different types of currency in circulation within the provinces (Bobango 1979, 85). With the new administration came new needs for revenue. These were answered by increased license fees and taxes that were not well received by the populace. Riots and demonstrations against the new regime began in late 1860. "Yet, order had to be maintained to show that the Romanians could manage their own house" (Bobango 1979, 99). Nevertheless, Cuza was able to secure the support of the Porte for full administrative union of the provinces in 1861, although the agreement would last only throughout his rule (Boia 1993, 7).

Serbia and Romania opened permanent diplomatic missions in 1863. Serbia was increasingly under pressure from the Ottomans and desired to unite the Balkan countries against the empire. Romania played a major role in this strategy and Serbia found a willing ally that provided arms to Serbia when others would not. Turkey suspected that the two states had formed a secret alliance against the empire. Cuza was forced to abdicate.

The Ottomans claimed that Cuza's abdication voided the unification of the provinces by agreement but this position did not gain the support of the guaranteeing powers. Nevertheless, the Romanian parliament understood the necessity of stability in developing its internal and external identities and moved quickly to fill the throne. A foreign prince, Charles of Hohenzollern-Sigmaringen, was brought in and proclaimed Prince Carol I in 1866. Once again, in recognition of their harmonies of interests, Serbia was the first to recognize the new leader. Carol I proceeded to forge the alliance between Romania and Serbia that the Ottomans had feared. In 1878, after failing to remain neutral, Romania joined with Russia and Serbia in the Russo-Turkish war. With their victory in the war, both Romania and Serbia gained full independence from the Ottoman Empire. Their mutual interests were sealed in the fact that they were trying to forge similar identities in the European system as important minor powers at the fringes of great power politics.

The end of World War I represented the next phase in the development of Romanian identity and in the close relationships between Romania and what would become Yugoslavia. Initially both countries remained neutral but each entered the conflict with the desire to extend their sovereignty to ethnic Romanians and Serbs that resided outside their borders. "Romania entered WWI to attain national unification. Its major irredentist objectives were Transylvania (including the Banat, Crisana, the Maramures) and the Bukovina, under Austria-Hungary, and Bessarabia, under Russia" (Boia 1993, 24).

In 1914 Romania had 7,700,000 people and a territory of 130,903 square kilometers. After the union of Transylvania, the Banat, the Bukovina, and Bessarabia, at the end of World War I, Greater Romania had approximately 16,500,000 people and a territory of 295,049 square kilometers. But unlike before the war when the country was overwhelmingly Romanian, Greater Romania now had large minority groups. (Boia 1993, 64)

The interwar period demanded a new phase of Romanian identity. No longer did Romania need to identify itself as the lone protector of the will

of the great powers in the Balkans. At the end of World War I, both countries had to forge new identities based on holding onto their gains from
the war. Again, they found themselves in harmony of interest, but this
time their enemies were all around them, for land had been ceded from
Austria, Russia, Hungary, and the Soviet Union. Friends were scarce in
the region, but at least they had each other.

> In foreign affairs, Romania's relations with its neighbors were precarious.
> In the process of national consolidation, with the exception of the Yugoslav
> state, neighboring countries had ceded to Romania significant territories,
> albeit inhabited by many Romanians. This fact did not endear Romania to
> its neighbors (i.e., Soviet Union, Hungary, Bulgaria) who became revisionist
> during the interwar period, clamoring for the redrawing of frontiers man-
> dated by the peace treaties. (Boia 1993, 65–66)

The relationship between Romania and Serbia/Yugoslavia was not
wholly without conflict. Yugoslavia, as a state, was formed through the
combination of many territories with Serbia in the Treaty of Paris that
ended World War I. The Banat region of Romania was one of the territories that was in dispute. Each of the two countries wanted the entire
region ceded unto itself. Romania favored a referendum within the territory to determine its fate as a whole.

> Having gone to Paris quarreling over the disposition of the Banat in 1919, the
> Romanians and Serbs came very close to the brink of military confrontation
> over this province. The representatives of the great powers at the peace con-
> ference, ignorant of the province's realities, made up their own rules based
> on their self-interests and eventually divided the Banat. (Boia 1993, 70)

As each of these newly consolidated states tried to reform its image in the
international system, the conflict over the Banat demonstrated that identities are not always created, they are sometimes received from the social
interactions of the system itself.

> Attempts were made at Paris to make a just peace but the Big Four had con-
> flicting objectives on many issues, from broad to narrow. The same situation
> existed for the smaller allies. In the end, national interests of the victorious
> great powers prevailed, whether it was on subjects of concern between them
> toward the defeated states, or toward their less powerful allies. (Boia 1993, 70)

Regardless of the vagaries of major power politics, both Romania
and Yugoslavia had to deal with threats that arose from an increasingly
unstable political situation in the peninsula in the interwar period. David Campbell (1998) points out that danger can be a powerful tool for
defining or redefining both internal and external identity. Romania and

Yugoslavia faced similar situations in defining identities as small states in a perilous region. As before World War I, each tried to establish its importance to the major powers—this time more through economic resources than through their strategic location—due in large part to the fall of the Ottoman Empire which diminished the strategic importance of the region to the other major powers. This led to a significant issue in the development of each state's international identity. Albert Hirschman's (1945) analysis of the influence effect of trade focused on the trading relationships between Nazi Germany and Southern Europe. As these states increased the concentration of their trading relationship with Germany, they gained from the supply effect trade but they also suffered from the influence effect. Romania, in particular, felt the pressures from the influence effect of trade through the 1930s.

> Relations with their neighbors determined the course Romania and Yugoslavia followed in their mutual association and in their affairs with great powers. The two pursued a policy designed to maintain the status quo established at Paris. When the western powers, the main pillars of the system, began to undermine this stand in the mid-1930s by embarking on an appeasement policy, they did not make a complete break, sending mixed signals to the east. Yugoslavia, sensing the necessity to improve relations with the revisionist great powers, slowly began to detach itself from this policy of maintaining the post-World War I settlements. (Boia 1993, 316)

Again, both states' options for action and their preferences for those options were tempered by their attempts to create an identity in the Europeans system. Those attempts to define their own identity, in the end, were overwhelmed by identities imposed on them by major power politics.

The third phase in the development of the Romanian identity began after World War II. The war began with Romania's greatest fears. In 1940, Russia demanded the cession of the Bessarabia and Bukovina regions (Keefe et al. 1972, 20). Other territorial concessions followed. These moves had a profound effect on Romanian internal politics. King Carol appointed a pro-German cabinet and the influence of the Iron Guard, a pro-German conservative movement, increased (Keefe et al. 1972, 21). Romania entered the war on the side of Germany against the Soviet Union in 1940. In August 1944, King Michael overthrew the pro-German regime and Romania re-entered the war on the side of the allies. In the armistice with the Allies, Romania agreed to pay war reparations and accepted military occupation by the Soviets (Keefe et al. 1972, 21). The Soviet Union used its occupation after World War II to fix elections and install a pro-Soviet regime. By December 1947, King Michael was forced to abdicate to avoid a civil war and Romania declared itself to be the Romanian People's Republic (Keefe et al. 1972, 23–24).

Romanian identity during the early years of the Cold War was pre-scribed through its relationships with the Soviet Union and the other communist states in the region. Identity was also strongly influenced by the image ascribed to the Eastern Bloc states by the rest of the world. This image of the subservient puppet state, however, was not always ac-curate and was particularly errant when applied to Romania. Romania began to cut its own path away from Soviet influence in 1963 in a dispute over Soviet plans to create a new planning board within COMECON that could directly affect investment and development projects in the member states. Romania rejected this proposal and began a program of "de-Sovietization" in which Soviet shops were closed, mandatory Rus-sian language courses in the schools were stopped, and streets that were named to honor Soviet heroes were returned to their original names. Ro-mania also began to forge an independent foreign policy by recognizing Albania, remaining neutral in the conflicts with China, and negotiating trade agreements with western countries (Keefe et al. 1972, 27).

Throughout this time, Romania once again found an ally of conve-nience in Yugoslavia. Yugoslav communism never fell under the rule of the Soviet Union and the neighbors found themselves again in concert in trying to create identities. Nevertheless, both countries found their at-tempts to create independent identities were overshadowed either by the identities forced upon them by external powers or by the images ascribed to them by the rest of the world. Again, these identities determined the range of options and the preferences for those options in both domestic and international affairs.

From the middle of the nineteenth century to the end of the twentieth century, Romania and Yugoslavia followed a similar path to create their identities. In the late 1800s both states had to create an independent identity through bargaining their geopolitical importance with the great powers. In the interwar period, they both found themselves struggling to maintain gains achieved during World War I in the face of increasing pressures from their neighbors and increasing isolation from the rest of the world. In the Cold War era, they once again found themselves forging similar identities as independent communist states in a world where com-munism was painted with a single brush. "Unlike the general situation in the region, Romania and Yugoslavia had few differences between them. Consequently, these two states sought each other out to collaborate for the maintenance of the territorial status quo" (Boia 1993, 316).

So, why, at the end of the Cold War, did Romania offer its airfields as a staging area for the most significant military action against Yugoslavia since the end of World War II? This question will be addressed in the next section through an analysis of Romania's decision to assist NATO in the Kosovo campaign. The answer lies not in the mechanics of strategic interaction, but in the utility preferences that Romania faced as it forged yet another identity at end of the Cold War.

ROMANIAN IDENTITY IN POST-COLD WAR EUROPE
AND THE KOSOVO CAMPAIGN

By 1989, President Nicolae Ceauşescu built a "Chinese Wall" around Romania—isolating it from both the East and West. Romania ignored reforms in the rest of central Europe and the revolution of 1989 took the Romanians by surprise (Cernicova-Buca 2001). Revolution began with the persecution of Lazlo Tokes, a pastor of Hungarian descent who called for political reforms. Tokes was exiled to a small town in northern Romania. His supporters staged a silent candlelight protest in Timisoara. Ceauşescu ordered the pacification of Timisoara, but the army sided with the protesters. As the revolt spread to other cities, including Bucharest, Ceauşescu and his wife fled. They were captured, tried, and executed. A National Salvation Front (NSF) was formed, mostly out of members of the communist party. The NSF proclaimed that it would uphold Romania's obligations to the Warsaw Pact, but within a year that pact was dissolved (Cernicova-Buca 2001, 199–201).

Romania, once again, had to forge a new identity. This time, the situation proved to be very difficult for the entire region had simultaneously experienced a transformation similar to Romania's. Hungary and Czechoslovakia had relatively peaceful transitions from communism. Ukraine was now a very large newly independent state on Romania's border with which Romania had no diplomatic history. Yugoslavia, its traditional ally in the region, was beginning to disintegrate. In the larger European system, Romania desired to integrate with the Western institutions that it had so bitterly opposed throughout the Cold War. This was a cold calculation based on its perception of the utility of those organizations.

> At the beginning of the twenty-first century, Romania's main goal is to ensure its admission into the two most successful international organizations in Europe, the North Atlantic Treaty Organization and the European Union. Both of these organizations provide a framework for general success and stability. The countries that belong to them enjoy enviable security and have a leading position in the world economy. In contrast, as the Cold War has faded away, the structures within which Romania had exerted its influence have dissolved, leaving behind only debts, bitterness, and insecurity. Thus, the aspiration to join NATO and the EU is not the latest fashion of the fin de siècle, but rather the necessary choice for success and progress in coming decades. (Cernicova-Buca 2001, 199)

But what would it take to redefine Romania as a Western power and was Romania ready to do this? The identity that Romania had to pursue was defined not by Romania, but by the Western powers it hoped to join. NATO opened the possibility of new membership when it announced the Partnership for Peace program in 1994. Romania was one of the first states to apply for provisional membership. The criteria for membership were laid out in the NATO enlargement study in September 1995 (NATO, 1995). They included six general conditions that prospective members would have to meet (Simon and Binnendijk 1997). These conditions were:

- Holding democratic elections and support for Individual liberty and the rule of law;
- A demonstrated commitment to economic reform and a market economy;
- Adherence to OSCE norms regarding treatment of minorities and social justice;
- Resolution of territorial disputes with neighbors;
- Democratic control of the military; and
- The new members would have to have the resources and commitment to creating NATO interoperability within their military.

Such was the identity that Romania had to pursue. From the start, Romanian candidacy was shaky. It lagged behind other Eastern European states in its reform efforts and it had little political constituency in the West (Simon and Binnendijk 1997). Romania was not included in the first round of NATO expansion countries at the Madrid Summit in 1997. However, a study by faculty at the United States National Defense University concluded that "Romania has made enough progress in political reforms and treatment of ethnic minorities to warrant consideration for NATO candidacy" (Simon and Binnendijk 1997, 1).

The NATO bombing campaign against the FRY, however, brought serious challenges to Romania's identity as a NATO candidate and to its identity as an ally of Yugoslavia. NATO asked Romania for use of their airfields and for overflight of their airspace. Should the new identity of Romania pursue this plan or should it support its ally of the last 140 years through neutrality?

The evolution of Romanian identity since 1853 had four phases and also had three major issues. First, Romania recognized that it needed to interact with the major powers of each era. Second, Romania was able to cut a somewhat independent path whether it was in its dealings with the Ottoman Porte, Nazi Germany, or Soviet Russia. Often this independent path had to succumb to major power interests, but Romania saw itself and was seen by others as a maverick. Finally, throughout its history of sovereignty, Romania linked its fate with Serbia/Yugoslavia. This was a marriage of convenience among relatively equal partners, but it served both of their needs. The Kosovo crisis was a challenge to this identity —especially the identity as an ally of Yugoslavia. In the end, as before, Romania's interplay with the major powers dominated the identity.

In a simplified model of the decision, Romania had two choices—to permit NATO to use its airfields and airspace or to deny that access. Figure 6.1 shows the decisions about use of the Romanian airfields and NATO membership as a 2 x 2 variables sum game. The preferences for the outcomes of this game are determined by the identities of the players in the situation of choice. Romania's best outcome would be to gain NATO membership without letting NATO use its airfields (cell c). This outcome would satisfy its dual identity as an independent ally of the FRY while establishing itself as a member of the larger European society of states. However, Romania perceived that NATO's decision about its membership was contingent on its choice regarding the use of airfields. In a letter to parliament, President Emil Constantinescu stated that "A neutral attitude would mean the end of the project of Romania joining NATO and the European Union" (Dow Jones 1999). Romania's next best outcome was to be rewarded with NATO membership for its offering the airfields (cell a). This would enhance Romania's identity as an important member of the European community, but it would deny Romania's identity as an independent ally of the FRY. While NATO membership may have been contingent on Romania's cooperation with the Kosovo campaign, it was unlikely that NATO would offer it as a quid pro quo. The outcome in cell b is less desirable but it leaves open the possibility of NATO membership in the future while denying NATO access to Romanian airfields would likely close that door (cell d). Romania's preference ordering in the game is Cell c > Cell a > Cell b > Cell d. NATO clearly preferred any outcome that permitted it to use Romania's airfields. It preferred not to have to make that use contingent on Romania's membership (Cell b > Cell a). If Romania denied access to the airfields, NATO certainly would not prefer to give Romania membership (Cell d > Cell c). NATO's preference ordering in the game is (Cell b > Cell a > Cell d > Cell c).

There are no dominated rows in the game but column II dominates column I. Given that NATO would choose not to link Romanian participation with its cooperation in the Kosovo campaign, Romania would still choose to allow NATO to the use its airfields. The natural outcome of this game is cell b with a value of 2,4.[1] This is also the unique Nash equilibrium. The natural outcome is a Pareto Optimal equilibrium but it is threat vulnerable. That is, if Romania threatened to deny use of its airfields, NATO would be inclined to offer membership in NATO as an incentive.

	NATO's Choices:	
Romania's Choices:	I. Approve Romania's Membership	II. Deny Romania's Membership
A. Permit NATO's use of Airfields	3,3* <div align="right">a</div>	<div align="right">b</div> [2,4] *
B. Deny NATO's use of Airfields	<div align="right">c</div> 4,1 *	d 1,2

Figure 6.1.   **The Romania–NATO normal form game.** *Source*: author.

The game, of course, has no predictive value because we know what happened. The proposal to assist NATO was hotly debated but, as Mariana Cernicova-Buca (2001, 211) put it, "Romanian policymakers chose Western solutions to the Kosovo crisis." In the end, the desire for NATO membership and to be identified with the major powers won out over other aspects of Romania's identity.

CONCLUSION

"Identity is an inescapable dimension of being. Nobody could be without it. Inescapable as it is, identity—whether personal or collective—is not fixed by nature, given by god, or planned by intentional behavior. Rather, identity is constituted in relation to difference. But neither is difference fixed by nature, given by god, or planned by intentional behavior. Difference is constituted in relation to identity. (Campbell 1998, 9)

Identity matters. It creates an image of the agent which is used by the agent as a shortcut for deciding what to do. The image is also used by others to decide how to respond to the actions of the agent. In doing so, the image becomes the agent—it constitutes the agent.

Romania was ever creating and recreating its identity. Sometimes that identity was created for it by others. In either case, the image of that identity became a guide for Romanian foreign policy decisions by identifying actions and by providing decision-makers with a sense of which of those actions would be appropriate for creating or reinforcing the identity. In this way the identity constructed rules. In the late nineteenth century, Romania forged an identity as a key player in an important part of the European map. This identity served it well as it emerged from World War I with significantly more land and resources than when the war began. The interwar period was less stable and less beneficial to Romania overall. Again, Romania attempted to project the identity of a key player in European politics. Unfortunately, European politics had, for the most part, moved beyond the Balkans. Romania was left struggling merely to maintain the positions it gained in World War I. Coming out of World War II, Romania's identity was given to it by the vagaries of the Cold War. Among its new allies, it was perceived as a client state, albeit one that tended to break away from the pact at times. Among the Western powers it was necessarily perceived as an enemy, regardless of its attempts at independent policy.

The Kosovo Crisis and the end of the Cold War threw Romania's key identities into conflict. It had to make a choice between its image as an independent among stronger players, its identity as an ally of Yugoslavia, and its desired identity as a member of NATO. In the end, major power politics won out again. At each step in this process, identity defined the state but it also defined the choices and provided utility guidance among those choices.

NOTE

1. In Rapoport and Guyer's taxonomy of 2 x 2 games, this game is game number 39.

SEVEN

Human Rights

Consensus, Norms, and Public Bads

> The future must see the broadening of human rights throughout the world. People who have glimpsed freedom will never be content until they have secured it for themselves. In a truest sense, human rights are a fundamental object of law and government in a just society. Human rights exist to the degree that they are respected by people in relations with each other and by governments in relations with their citizens.
>
> Eleanor Roosevelt (1948)

THE CONSTRUCTION OF HUMAN RIGHTS IN WESTERN HISTORY AND PHILOSOPHY

In order for something to be a public good, it must first be a good. That is, it must be perceived to provide increased utility through at least some range of additional supply. Eleanor Roosevelt's quotation implies that human rights are goods, but this has not always been the case. The quotation is from a speech that Mrs. Roosevelt gave at the Sorbonne in 1948 when she was the chairperson of the United Nations Commission on Human Rights. It is an impassioned plea that the world accept that human rights embodied in the Universal Declaration of Human Rights are global public goods.

The modern Western tradition of human rights deriving from some quality of being human emerged from two late eighteenth century documents: the French Declaration of the Rights of Man and of the Citizen (1789) and the U.S. Bill of Rights (1791). James Griffin claims that these documents embody the concept of human rights that informs us today and there has been little change in this conception from the late eighteenth century definition as "a right we simply have in virtue of being human, with no further explanation of what human means" (Griffin 2008, 13). Both of these documents relied on the claim of human rights being self-evident, which is odd because "if equality of rights is so self-evident, they why did this assertion have to be made and why was it only made in specific times and places?" (Hunt 2007, 19). Lynn Hunt claims that the self-evidence of human rights emerged out of the enlightenment ideals of autonomy and empathy. She notes that

> social and political change—in this case, human rights—comes about be-
> cause many individuals had similar experiences, not because they all inhab-
> ited the same social context but because through their interactions with each
> other and with their reading and viewing, they actually created a new social
> context. In short, I am insisting that any account of historical change must in
> the end account for the alteration of individual minds. For human rights to
> become self-evident, ordinary people had to have new understandings that
> came from new kinds of feelings. (Hunt 2007, 34)

These understandings, according to Hunt, were constructed in part through the literature of the day, especially published accounts of torture and the epistolary novel. Changing hearts and minds, however, was a slow process. Hunt recounts the effect of Voltaire's *Treatise on Tolerance on the Occasion of the Death of Jean Calas* that was published in 1763. Calas was condemned to torture and execution for killing his son to prevent him from converting to Catholicism, although evidence indicated his son committed suicide. Voltaire was credited with changing French views on torture, although his book focused more on the wrongful conviction than the horrible fate that befell Calas before his death. Torture continued to be used throughout Europe through the end of the eighteenth century. The British Bill of Rights of 1689 prohibited cruel punishment, although many of the convicted continued to be subjected to extreme measures. As Hunt points out, "What constituted 'cruel' punishments depended on cultural expectations" (Hunt 2007, 77).

The nineteenth century saw an expansion of the application and guarantee of human rights in Western politics through three mass move-ments—the expansion of the liberal democratic state, the expansion of suffrage, and the expanding international norm against and subsequent banning of the slave trade. The nineteenth century also brought about the first major international convention that asserted the role of human rights over sovereign rights in the first Geneva Convention of 1864.

During the twentieth century, human rights evolved from concepts that defined the nature of the liberal state to universal values that transcend national boundaries. This evolution is evident in the rising importance of intergovernmental organizations and was accelerated by the horrible vio-lations of human rights during two world wars. The twentieth century also saw the promotion of human rights encounter resistance in the protection of state sovereignty as human rights became more internationalized. Yet, this justification of sovereign rights over human rights was instrumental in justifying the first and most important document specifying the universality of human rights of the modern era—the United Nations Universal Declaration of Human Rights (hereafter the Universal Declaration). The Universal Declaration would never have gained acceptance had it not been for the horrors of World War II. The Universal Declaration was not a treaty with binding obligations. It was, instead, a statement of universally accepted norms. The norms of the Universal Declaration (1948) were later codified in two United Nations treaties—the International Covenant on Civil and Political Rights (ICCPR) along with its two optional protocols, and the International Covenant on Economic, Social and Cultural Rights (ICESCR). These documents form the so-called International Bill of Rights (UNHCHR 2010a). Seven other United Nations treaties on human rights have been negotiated, signed, and enacted (see UNHCHR 2010b). Thus, a United Nations regime for protecting human rights has been well defined through the United Nations Charter, the Universal Declaration, nine core UN human rights treaties, various General Assembly and Council resolutions, and other multilateral treaties. This regime and similar regional regimes have gained general acceptance within the international system. As David Forsythe stated in the opening article of a symposium reviewing fifty years of the Universal Declaration:

The dominant pattern is that states pay lip service to human rights. They sign human rights treaties even if they have no intention of shaping their policies and restricting their power according to the terms of the treaties. There is thus a broad, if shallow, consensus that states—even in anarchical international relations—should respect the individual and collective rights of persons. (Forsythe 1998, 508)

Susan Mendus points out that everyone agrees with the shallow consensus that human rights should be protected, everyone, that is, except philosophers (Mendus 1995, 10). The philosophical debate continues to rage regarding the nature and even the existence of human rights. Jeremy Bentham famously claimed that

Natural rights is simple nonsense: natural and imprescriptible rights, rhetorical nonsense, nonsense upon stilts. But this rhetorical nonsense ends in the old strain of mischievous nonsense. For immediately a list of these pretended natural rights is given, and these are so expressed as to present to view legal rights. And of these rights, whatever they are, there is not, it seems, any one of which any government *can* (in the cut-throat sense of the word *can*) *can* upon any occasion whatever abrogate the smallest particle. (Bentham 2011, 328)

This inability to ensure the protection of unalienable rights led Alistair MacIntyre to proclaim that the truth is plain: there are no such rights, and belief in them is one with belief in witches and in unicorns.

The best reason for asserting so bluntly that there are no such rights is indeed of precisely the same type as the best reason which we possess for asserting that there are no witches and the best reason which we possess for asserting that there are no unicorns: every attempt to give good reasons for believing that there are such rights has failed. (MacIntyre 2007, 69)

Other philosophers, like Forsythe, believe that universal human rights do exist simply because they are broadly recognized to exist by nation-states. Steven Lukes claims that

> The principle that human rights must be defended has become one of the commonplaces of our age. Sometimes the universality of human rights has been challenged: those historically proclaimed are said to be Eurocentric and to be inappropriate, or only partly appropriate, to other cultures and circumstances.
>
> So alternative, or partly alternative, lists are proposed. Sometimes the historic lists are said to be too short, and so further human rights are proposed, from the second unto the third and fourth generation. Sometimes the appeal to human rights, or the language in which it is couched, are said to be unhelpful or even counterproductive in particular campaigns or struggles—in advancing the condition and position of women, say, or in promoting Third World development. But virtually no-one actually rejects the principle of defending human rights. (Lukes 1994, 111)

Lukes also points out that while protection of human rights is proclaimed everywhere, they are also violated nearly everywhere. Schachter (1982, 336) believes that most of the provisions of the Universal Declaration have entered the realm of customary international law due to the generalized acceptance of human rights norms. James Nickel, however, does not believe that "enough moral agreement exists worldwide to support anything like the full range of rights declared in contemporary manifestos" (Nickel 2007, 46).

One of the major concerns is that universal human rights suffers from cultural relativism. Human rights are culturally relative when they are defined by local custom, tradition, religion, or culture rather than by a universally established standard. Cultural relativism means that human rights cannot be universally applied but must be determined by the culturally accepted practice of each society (Teson 1985, 870–871). The American Anthropology Association raised this concern before the United Nations voted on the Universal Declaration, asking the UN Human Rights Commission, "How can the proposed Declaration be applicable to all human beings, and not be a statement of rights conceived only in terms of the values prevalent in the countries of Western Europe and America?"

(American Anthropological Association 1947, 539). Their statement on human rights concluded that "Only when a statement of the right of men to live in terms of their own traditions is incorporated into the proposed Declaration, then, can the next step of defining the rights and duties of human groups as regards each other be set upon the firm foundation of the present-day scientific knowledge of Man" (543). Tracy Higgins (1996, 92) notes that, in the wake of the Nazi Holocaust, world leaders found the cultural relativism critique troubling and explicitly embraced the values of universal human rights in the UN document. This was not the end of the debate. Concerns about cultural relativism and the protection of sovereign rights were raised over the next forty-five years as the United Nations debated and passed more specific resolutions and covenants defining universal human rights. These concerns coalesced into the Bangkok Declaration that resulted from the Regional Meeting for Asia of the World Conference on Human Rights where thirty-five Asian, South Asian, and Middle Eastern states asserted that "while human rights are universal in nature, they must be considered in the context of a dynamic and evolving process of international norm-setting, bearing in mind the significance of national and regional particularities and various historical, cultural and religious backgrounds" (Singhvi 1993, 5).

The Bangkok Declaration voiced concerns about universal human rights based on Asian values in contrast to the Western values embedded in the Universal Declaration. Jack Donnelly points out that these contrasts can enhance the view of universal rights rather than challenge them. He notes that human rights allow people to choose what is best for their situation. "If Asians truly do value family over self, they will exercise their personal rights with the consequences for their family in mind. If they value harmony and order, they will exercise their civil liberties in a harmonious and orderly fashion" (Donnelly 2003, 122). Universal human rights do not demand that people abandon their culture. In Donnelly's words, they "represent the international community's best effort to define the social and political parameters of our common humanity" (Donnelly 2003, 123).

It may be possible to reach consensus on the existence of rights even if there is no consensus about their philosophical foundation (see Freeman 1994, 493 commenting on Lomasky 1987, 13). The consensus about the existence of rights serves a function in society.

> A community of such rights holders, secure in their own status and prepared to recognize the comparable status of others, will be a community infrequently riven by divisive clashes. The common recognition of rights eliminates areas of potential conflict that bedevil a society in which rights are less visible or altogether unrecognized. (Lomasky 1987, 15)

For Charles Beitz, this consensus represents a discursive and political practice that has emerged in international law, intergovernmental institutions, foreign policies, and non-governmental institutions (Beitz 2009, 1). The practice exists as a set of norms and strategies that give agents reasons to act. (Beitz 2009, 8–9). In the context of a utility-based model of public goods, these reasons derive, in part, from the identity of the agent. Jack Donnelly discusses the importance of human rights in national identity at length. He notes that human rights were at the center of the justification of the formation of states such as the United States, France, and many states in Latin America. Colonial powers such as Great Britain and the Netherlands adopted identities as protectors of human rights as their empires dissipated (Donnelly 2013, 199–200). Donnelly also claims that regional and international organizations and non-governmental organizations play a role in incorporating human rights in national identities. For example, Article F.2 of the Treaty on European Union (Maastricht Treaty) requires members to respect those rights guaranteed under the European Convention for the Protection of Human Rights and Fundamental Freedoms (European Union 1992). This commitment to the protection of human rights is strengthened in the Charter of Fundamental Rights of the European Union that came into force in 2009. The Charter refers to the EU's "spiritual and moral heritage" as the foundation of its "indivisible, universal values of human dignity, freedom, equality and solidarity" (European Union 2000, 8). It reaffirms the EU's commitment to the human rights obligations specified in prior European treaties. European Union members and states seeking membership are obliged to acquire the identity of protectors of human rights under the terms of these treaties.

THE UNIVERSAL DECLARATION OF HUMAN RIGHTS: PUBLIC GOODS BY CONSENSUS

David Forsythe (1998) believes that the international system has accepted a broad consensus that human rights should be protected. As an example, he notes that no state joined the UN while placing a reserve on Articles 55 and 56 of the Charter that require members to cooperate in protecting human rights. On December 10, 1948, the Universal Declaration of Human Rights passed in the General Assembly by a vote of forty-eight in favor with eight abstentions and no votes against the resolution. The eight states that abstained (the Soviet Bloc, Saudi Arabia, and South Africa) disagreed with the Declaration, but none voted against it. Since the Declaration passed, seven of the eight states that abstained renounced their abstentions. Only Saudi Arabia has remained resolute in not affirming the Declaration, due primarily to the Declaration's statement that men and women have the same rights to marry. The utility-based model of public goods helps explain how this event led to the global consensus on human rights principles.

The great powers showed little interest in the protection of human rights during the meetings at Dumbarton Oaks and San Francisco to establish the United Nations. China, France, Great Britain, the United States, and the Soviet Union were concerned with winning the war and securing the postwar peace. Many of the smaller states in the rest of world faced a postwar world still under the thumb of European colonial powers. These nations, supported by a unified block of Latin American states, pushed for an explicit statement of human rights in the UN Charter and a human rights commission to be established within the Economic and Social Council of the UN. The United States relented on the idea of the commission but stood firm against an explicit bill of human rights, due to what the bill would imply about its own race relations (Glendon 2001, 10–18). The United States may have yielded to the pressure of the coalition, but it also saw an opportunity to use an official role for human rights as a tool in its increasing tension with the Soviet Union. Ultimately, the UN Charter included specific references to human rights in the Preamble, and Articles 1, 13, 55, 56, 62, 68, 73, and 76. Article 56 explicitly requires member states to "take joint and separate action" to achieve the purposes of "universal respect for, and observance of, human rights and fundamental freedoms for all without distinction as to race, sex, language, or religion" that are set forth in Article 55. Article 68 calls for the creation of a commission on human rights. The UN Human Rights Commission was established by the Third Committee of the General Assembly in 1946 under the Economic and Social Council. It was renamed as the UN Human Rights Council in 2006. The Third Committee recommended that the first project of the Human Rights Commission was to create a bill of human rights, which would become the Universal Declaration (Glendon 2001, 31).

The Universal Declaration grew out of the horrors of the Holocaust and the Second World War. Johannes Morsink drove this point home in the second chapter of his book where he documented the specific events of the war that the drafters used to justify adopting each article in the Declaration.

> The motif that runs throughout these adoptions and rejections is that the Universal Declaration was adopted to avoid another Holocaust or similar abomination . . . While they often differed on the specific wording to be used, once it was shown that a violation of a certain clause or article had in some way helped create the horrors of the war, the adoption of that clause or article was virtually assured (Morsink 1999, 37).

John P. Humphrey, a Canadian legal scholar and the director of the UN Secretariat's Human Rights Division, wrote the first draft of the Universal

Declaration. Humphrey presented a draft that he said, "included every conceivable right" (quoted from the Drafting Committee minutes by Glendon 2001, 57). The Drafting Committee thought the Humphrey draft was too sweeping and unorganized. They decided to create a smaller working group of four members that included Eleanor Roosevelt from the United States, René Cassin from France, Charles Malik from Lebanon, and Geoffrey Wilson from Great Britain. Cassin was tasked with rewriting the draft (See Glendon 2001, chapter 4 and Morsink 1999, 5–6). An expanded eight-member Drafting Committee reviewed and revised the draft and presented it to the whole Human Rights Commission in Geneva in December, 1947. Fourteen of the rest of the forty-eight members of the United Nations responded to the Geneva draft (Morsink 1999, 10). Most of the concerns about the draft that dominated the Drafting Committee's second meeting in May, 1948, related to whether the final document was to be a declaration of principles or a binding covenant. These issues also dominated the June, 1948, meeting of the full Human Rights Commission. The disagreements were so severe that the delegates ultimately agreed to postpone discussion of a covenant and its implementation and proceed with the declaration of principles (Morsink 2001, 10–11).

The Universal Declaration was finally presented to the full General Assembly during its third meeting in the fall of 1948. The Third Committee of the General Assembly held eighty-five meetings on the Declaration from September to December of 1948. Charles Malik, chairman of the Third Committee, stated that 88 percent of the 1,233 votes cast during this process were affirmative votes (UNGA 1948, 860). The USSR, supported by the rest of the Soviet Bloc, proposed to table the discussion until the next General Assembly meeting to allow the Commission to rewrite the Declaration. They were concerned that the Declaration weakened sovereignty and that it contained no language that clearly defined the rights of the state as opposed to the rights of the individual. It appeared that the Soviet Bloc would vote against the Declaration, which would be a blow to the desire by many to have universal agreement. A total of thirty-four of the fifty-eight members of the UN spoke during the debate over the next day and a half. Of the thirty-four speakers, seven spoke against the Declaration (Byelorussia, Czechoslovakia, Poland, South Africa, Ukraine, USSR, and Yugoslavia). The rest of the speakers praised the Declaration, while noting its flaws. Some compared it to the Magna Carta, the French Declaration of the Rights of Man, and the American Bill of Rights. Mr. Santa Cruz of Chile declared that "Henceforth, men everywhere would know what their rights and freedoms were" (UNGA 1948, 863). There was a general call for support among the speakers. Eleanor Roosevelt of the United States noted that the Universal Declaration represented a compromise and that it did not contain all of what the United States had wished. She remarked that "people sometimes had to co-operate loyally with the majority even when they disagreed with its views." In the end, no member state voted against the Universal Declaration. It passed by a vote of forty-eight in favor, eight abstentions, and two no-votes.[1] Consensus was achieved.

Christoph Haug (2015) discusses two types of consensus phenomena. Cognitive or mental consensus refers to having similar orientations or attitudes toward something. It consists of shared understandings and perceptions. Performative or interactional consensus is based on Urfalino's rule of non-opposition.

> Following this rule, a participant of a meeting discussing a particular matter advances a proposition to be decided upon. In the case of an absence of contestation or counter-propositions, this proposition is deemed to be "accepted" and has conferred upon it the status of "decision" of that group. (Urfalino 2014, 321)

Haug points out that obtaining performative consensus through this rule of non-opposition does not necessarily mean that cognitive consensus has been achieved. From this, he also concludes that consensus is not the same as unanimity. Thus, it is possible for a proposal to lack opposition without obtaining a meeting of the minds.

In this regard, the Universal Declaration obtained consensus among the members of the United Nations on December 10, 1948, with the vote of forty-eight in favor, none opposed, and eight abstentions. This was a fragile consensus that was severely tested later as the issue of human rights moved from a declaration of principles to attempts to create covenants that implemented those principles. If anything, the cognitive consensus about the principles of human rights strengthened over time while challenges to state sovereignty weakened the performative consensus.

Consensus is a socially constructed decision process. It occurs in a complex web of social, psychological, cultural, historical, and political variables. The influence of these variables is hotly debated in the literature. Psychologically, consensus is the result of social persuasion. Subtle and not-so-subtle positive and negative pressures push and pull the participants into line with the emerging consensus. One means for these pressures is the principle of social proof, also referred to as the principle of consensus. Quite simply, people agree to do what other people do if they believe the action to be valid (Cialdini 2001, 2008). In a social setting, agreement tends to breed agreement. Individuals begin to take on the group identity as more and more members join the consensus. This bandwagon effect can increase the utility of an individual deciding whether or not to contribute to the provision of a public good, such as the protection of human rights, as illustrated in figure 7.1.

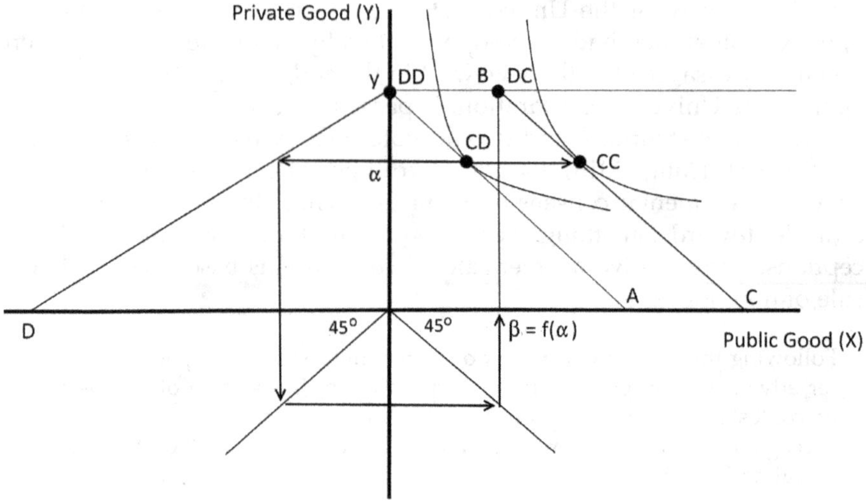

Figure 7.1.   Bandwagon effect of consensus on human rights principles.
Source: author.

Figure 7.1 shows an individual agent with the privileged preference ordering. In the other utility models in this book, the quantity of public good provided by the rest of the collective (β) is a function of the individual's subjective probability that the collective will provide x units of public good. In Figure 7.1, the amount of public good provided by the rest of the collective is determined by the bandwagon function graphed in the upper left quadrant of the figure. Although the bandwagon function is linear in figure 7.1, it could take on any form. The lines at 45° from the origin in the lower left and lower right quadrants translate the value from the bandwagon function back into the upper right quadrant to show how the amount of public good provided by the rest of the collective is a function of the amount of public good provided by the individual. Thus, as the individual provides more public good along line yA, the bandwagon function translates the CD outcome to line $\overline{BC}$ at outcome CC. In this way, the individual's decision to contribute enhances the collective's consensus to provide the good as well. Others do what the individual does, which is the essence of Cialdini's consensus principle of persuasion (see Cialdini 2001 and 2008 and Kaptien et al. 2009).

HUMAN RIGHTS AS A GLOBAL NORM

Martha Finnemore defines norms as "as shared expectations about appropriate behavior held by a community of actors" (Finnemore 1996, 22).

In addition to invoking a sense of what should or should not be done through the concept of appropriate behavior, Finnemore's definition establishes a quantitative characteristic of norms. It is this characteristic that sets norms apart from rules. Norms are a subset of rules. Not all rules are norms. To be a norm, the sense of what should or should not be done must be shared among a sufficient number of the agents in a community. Unlike a rule that can be dictated by one agent in authority, a norm is created when a sufficient number of agents agree that it affects behavior. This means that a norm must first be created and then disseminated before it comes into force.

Mona Krook and Jacqui True (2012, 106–109) review four different models of norm creation and dissemination in the literature. The "world polity model" (Meyer et al. 1997) proposes that nation-states are embedded in a world society with its own established culture and structure. Norms are generated exogenously. "States comply as a means to increase or enhance their international reputation and identity as 'modern' states" (Krook and True 2012, 107). In the "norm life cycle" model (Finnemore and Sikkink 1998), norms are created by norm entrepreneurs that promote them through various organizational platforms until the number of adherents reaches a tipping point. At this point the norm cascades through the society until it is instantiated by the community at large and becomes a taken-for-granted statement about appropriate behavior. The "boomerang model" proposed by Keck and Sikkink (1998) examines the cases where governments do not respond to civil society demands for changes in norms. The norm is promoted, instead, by transnational advocacy groups that "connect to transnational allies, who use the power of principled ideas and norms to lobby their own states or international organizations to put pressure on the recalcitrant state from the outside" (Krook and True 2012, 107). Finally, the "spiral model" builds on the boomerang model to examine how recalcitrant states are pressured to accept an international norm. The model proposes that the process goes through five stages of domestic repression, state denial, tactical concessions, prescriptive status, and rule-consistent behavior (Risse and Sikkink 1999). Among these four models, the Norm Life Cycle provides the greatest insight into how identities establish agents' preferences for adhering to an international norm.

Finnemore and Sikkink (1998) propose that norms are created and disseminated in three stages. In the first stage, norm emergence, norm entrepreneurs promote the norm by working with organizational platforms, such as civil society organizations or government agencies, using methods of persuasion. The first stage ends at the tipping point where a critical mass of agents adopts the norm and become norm leaders. While this threshold point is determined, in part, by sheer numbers, it also matters who the norm leaders are. A small number of influential agents can have as much effect on the tipping point as a large number of less significant agents. The second stage, the norm cascade, is when more agents rapidly adopt the norm through bandwagoning (Krook and True 2012, 107). Finnemore and Sikkink attribute this change to a "process of international socialization intended to induce norm breakers to become norm followers" and that agents "comply with norms in stage 2 for reasons that relate to their identities as members of an international society" (Finnemore and Sikkink 1998, 902). The norm affects the social dimension of the agent's utility where it gains social benefit through legitimacy, conformity, and esteem. Internalization, the final stage in the norm life cycle, occurs when norms "become so widely accepted that they are internalized by actors and achieve a "taken-for-granted" quality that makes conformance with the norm almost automatic" (Finnemore and Sikkink 1998, 904).

A norm can be conceptualized as a public good. The norm is nonexcludable if any compliance with the norm benefits society, regardless of whether or not any individual agents follows the norm. Since norms are typically ideational rather than material, they are, by nature, indivisible.

Kofi Annan, secretary-general of the United Nations, was disturbed by the 1994 Rwandan genocide and the NATO bombing of Serbia during the Kosovo intervention. In 1999, he challenged the member states to develop a consensus about when military intervention is appropriate to stop human rights abuses. "If, in those dark days and hours leading up to the genocide, a coalition of States had been prepared to act in defense of the Tutsi population, but did not receive prompt Council authorization, should such a coalition have stood aside and allowed the horror to unfold?" (Annan 1999, 2). Annan reiterated the challenge in his millennium report to the General Assembly in 2000 with the question, "I would pose this question: if humanitarian intervention is, indeed, an unacceptable assault on sovereignty, how should we respond to a Rwanda, to a Srebrenica—to gross and systematic violations of human rights that offend every precept of our common humanity?" (Annan 2000, 48). Out of this question arose the international norm that is now known as the Responsibility to Protect (R2P). Secretary General Ban Ki-moon (UNGA 2009), identified that R2P stood on three pillars of responsibilities in the face of systematic human rights abuses. First, it is the responsibility of each state to protect its citizens. Second, it is the responsibility of the international community to provide assistance to states, when needed, to halt human rights abuses. Finally, it is the responsibility of the international community to intervene, when authorized by the Security Council, to stop massive human rights abuses when the state is unable or unwilling to do so on its own.

11

Melissa Labonte (2016) traced the path of the Responsibility to Protect through the Finnemore and Sikkink's three stages of norm development. Initially, Annan's challenge was not well accepted among members of the Non-Aligned Movement who saw it as a threat to their sovereignty (Carter and Malone 2016, 285). Luke Glanville argues that R2P is not a substantial threat to sovereign autonomy.

> The present-day idea that sovereign states are responsible to their populations and to international society for the protection of individual rights does not break with a centuries-old tradition of unaltered and untrammeled sovereign rights. The boundaries of legitimate sovereign action have always been contested, and the idea that states have responsibilities—including a responsibility to protect the safety of individuals—has been an enduring feature of the discussion of legitimate sovereignty since it first emerged in the sixteenth and seventeenth centuries. (Glanville 2014, 9)

The concept of sovereignty as responsibility got a major boost with the publication of a Brookings Institution book entitled *Sovereignty as Responsibility: Conflict Management in Africa* (Deng et al. 1996). Amatai Etzioni captured the authors' thesis well when he said,

> when nations do not conduct their internal affairs in ways that meet internationally recognized standards, other nations not only have the right, but also have a duty, to intervene. Deng et al. propose that those governments that do not fulfill their responsibilities to their people forfeit their sovereignty. In effect, the authors redefine sovereignty as the responsibility to protect the people in a given territory. (Etzioni 2006, 271)

Canada was the first state to rise to Annan's challenge. Canada, with the assistance of the UN Secretariat, created the International Commission on Intervention and State Sovereignty (ICISS). The ICISS released its report in 2001. Kofi Annan created a High Level Panel on Threats Challenges and Change to consider the report and make recommendations for implementing R2P.

Finnemore and Sikkink (1998, 895) note that "The characteristic mechanism of the first stage, norm emergence, is persuasion by norm entrepreneurs. Norm entrepreneurs attempt to convince a critical mass of states (norm leaders) to embrace new norms." Labonte (2016, 137) identified many individuals that acted as norm entrepreneurs for R2P, including Kofi Annan, Gareth Evans, Ban Ki Moon, Francis Deng, Roberta Cohen, and Tony Blair. "Effective norm entrepreneurs spotlight and create issues, interpret and dramatize information, and engage in cognitive framing that ideally will resonate with other policy elites" (Labonte 2016, 137). In short, they take on the task of convincing agents to shift their identity toward accepting the norm and thereby shifting the agent's preference ordering to favor the public good.

A tipping point is reached once a sufficient body of states accept the norm. Labonte (2016, 136) believes that R2P has reached the tipping point.

> By all accounts, the human rights and humanitarian norms that constitute R2P—as linked to state's primary responsibility to protect, have, indeed, "tipped." Nearly all states are contracting parties to the Genocide Convention, signatories to all four of the 1949 Geneva Conventions, and endorse the Universal Declaration of Human Rights. Hundreds of states have ratified the International Covenant on Civil and Political Rights, and 123 nations are States Parties to the Rome Statute of the International Criminal Court.

The tipping point for R2P very likely came at the 2005 United Nations World Summit where 150 states accepted by proclamation that "Each individual State has the responsibility to protect its populations from genocide, war crimes, ethnic cleansing and crimes against humanity" (UNGA 2005, Section 138) and that

> we are prepared to take collective action, in a timely and decisive manner, through the Security Council, in accordance with the Charter, including Chapter VII, on a case-by-case basis and in cooperation with relevant regional organizations as appropriate, should peaceful means be inadequate and national authorities are manifestly failing to protect their populations from genocide, war crimes, ethnic cleansing and crimes against humanity. (UNGA 2005, Section 139)

Once a norm tips, it then cascades through the states. Finnemore and Sikkink characterize this as the beginning of the states shifting their identities. "What happens at the tipping point is that enough states and enough critical states endorse the new norm to redefine appropriate behavior for the identity called 'state'" (Finnemore and Sikkink 1998, 902). Labonte claims that R2P shows signs of cascading because of the number of times the Security Council has based resolutions on R2P and the number of times that R2P has been referenced in mandates for UN peacekeeping missions in the decade following the World Summit (Labonte 2016, 137). Hafner-Burton et al. (2008) provide more evidence of cascading human rights norms. In a cross-national time-series analysis, they showed that states with repressive human rights records ratified human rights treaties at the same rate as states with non-repressive human rights records. They ratify these treaties in an attempt to shift their identities in the eyes of other states and domestic interest groups (Hafner-Burton et al. 2008, 116).

The final stage of norm development is internalization. In this stage, norms are taken for granted and following the norm becomes automatic

(Finnemore and Sikkink 1998, 904). Labonte is skeptical that R2P has reached this stage yet. "It would be difficult to make the claim that R2P is an internalized norm—the intense and ongoing debates surrounding it suggest that R2P remains a contested set of norms" (Labonte 2016, 137).

The process of the Responsibility to Protect becoming a norm can be modeled with the utility-based model of public goods. Initially, in the norm emergence stage of the norm life-cycle, most agents would have the latent preference ordering for the norm that was shown in figure 3.5. The flat indifference curves indicate an agent that has little interest in providing the public good by complying with the norm. The rationalist approach to encouraging norm compliance is represented by Mancur Olson's selective incentive where a side payment is made to lower the cost of the public good relative to the numeraire or a selective punishment that raises the cost of non-compliance.

Constructivists approach the latent preferences of agents in stage 1 by shifting the identities of the agents through persuasion and the activities of the norm entrepreneurs. Carmen Wunderlich captures this process well.

> Invoking a logic of appropriateness instead, constructivists attribute to norms explanatory power for actors' behavior as they influence both the formation and change of actors' preferences and identities . . . Norm adherence results not from external sanctions or coercion but from a feeling of obligation and "oughtness" (Finnemore and Sikkink 1998, 891)—actors follow normative prescriptions because their identity tells them to do so. (Wunderlich 2013, 22)

As the agent's identity shifts, its utilities also shift to favor the public good of the norm. The norm life-cycle for an individual agent is a process of transformation of its public goods preferences from a latent or intermediate preference ordering in stage 1 to a privileged preference ordering in stage 3. In the utility-based model of public goods, this means that the utility curves become steeper, as shown by the dotted indifference curves in figure 7.2. The agent participates in the norm because its utilities shift to the privileged preference ordering as its identity as a norm follower shifts.

Alex Bellamy (2010) sees R2P as a set of norms, each relating to one of the three pillars of responsibility. There is general acceptance that the first pillar, that states have the responsibility to protect their own citizens, has cascaded and is in the process of being internalized. The success of the other two pillars, that the international community is responsible for assisting states protecting their citizens and that the international community has the responsibility to intervene when states are unable or unwilling to protect their citizens, has been inconsistent. The successful NATO intervention in Libya in 2011 is contrasted with the ongoing human rights disasters in Syria and Yemen. Luke Glanville (2016, 196–197)

Private Good (Y)

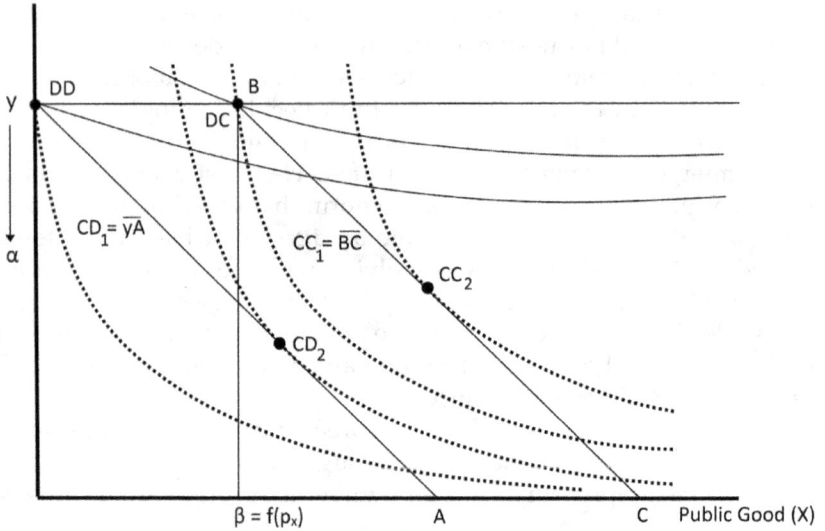

Figure 7.2.   Shift in utilities for a norm from stage 1 (solid) to stage 3 (dotted).
Source: author.

holds out hopes for these norms, pointing out successful attempts to assist
states protection of human rights in Côte d'Ivoire in 2011, Mali in 2012,
the Central African Republic in 2013, and Iraq in 2014 and noting that

> since the unanimous endorsement of R2P by states at the UN World Summit
> in 2005, there has been only one clear case, Libya, in which it was widely
> agreed that non-consensual intervention would be an effective and justifiable
> response to mass atrocities and, in that case, the international community did
> not fail to intervene.

WHEN HUMAN RIGHTS ARE PERCEIVED AS A PUBLIC BAD

Decisions are often influenced by the way that information about the
decision is perceived by the decision-maker. Tversky and Kahneman
referred to this process as the framing of decisions. "The frame that a
decision-maker adopts is controlled partly by the formulation of the problem and partly by the norms, habits, and personal characteristics of the
decision-maker" (Tversky and Kahneman 1981, 453). Their experimental
work demonstrated that decision-makers' preferences and choices could
be reversed, depending on how the context of a decision is presented.
Chong and Druckman call this type of frame an "individual frame" that
"refers to an individual's cognitive understanding of a given situation."
They compare it to a "media frame" that refers to the "images, phrases,

and presentation styles" that an opinion leader uses when discussing a decision (Chong and Druckman 2007, 100–101). Both types of decision frames affected the nascent consensus on human rights in the years after the Universal Declaration.

Charnysh et al. (2015) claim that decision framing was largely responsible for the consensus that emerged in agreements to prohibit human trafficking in recent years. They contend that framing human trafficking as a problem of crime prevention instead of a human rights issue increased the consensual support for the Protocol to Prevent, Suppress and Punish Trafficking in Persons (TIP Protocol) that was adopted in 2000. The TIP Protocol has been ratified by more than 150 states and 140 states have criminalized trafficking for sex and labor (Charnysh et al. 2015, 326).

As the Cold War unfolded in the early 1950s, identities of the major powers shifted. This caused the problems of implementing human rights protections to be reframed from the high-minded ideals intended to prevent a recurrence of the Holocaust to the Cold War sensibilities of superpower surrogate conflict. The consensus was threatened as human rights turned from a moral asset to a political liability. This shift can be demonstrated by the utility-based model of public goods and is evident in the United States response to the implementation of the International Covenant for Civil and Political Rights.

Initially, Eleanor Roosevelt hoped that the Universal Declaration would be a binding covenant. That hope was gone by the time the UN Human Rights Commission completed a draft for the General Assembly debate. She realized that her own U.S. Senate would not approve a binding agreement. She, and the other delegates, chose to create a declaration of principles and to ask the UN to charge the Commission and ECOSOC to develop a covenant for implementation of human rights as a next step (Glendon 2001 71–72). The draft of the covenant was presented to the General Assembly in the fall of 1950 (UN Resolution A/RES/421 [V]). The draft was hotly debated during the Third Committee meetings in 1951. The most controversial issue was a proposal by the United States to separate the draft into two covenants—one to address civil and political rights and the other to address economic, social, and cultural rights. Support for this proposal divided along both economic and political lines. The industrialized states of Europe and close Western Hemisphere allies of the United States supported the proposal while the Soviet Bloc and non-aligned states opposed it. The supporters expressed concern that economic, cultural, and social problems depend on the local culture and economy. The states that opposed the proposal claimed that separating the covenant denied the validity of economic, cultural, and social rights and diluted the idea that human rights were universal. How could human rights be universal if they can be parsed out and approved or denied in separate covenants? Nevertheless, the UN General Assembly passed the resolution to sever the covenant on February 5, 1952 by a vote of twenty-seven in favor, twenty against, and seven abstentions (UN Resolution A/RES/543/[VI]). Drafts of the two covenants were submitted to the General Assembly in 1954. As Christian Tomuschat notes,

> In an age of rising tensions between East and West during the time of the Cold War (1947–91), it was impossible to make rapid headway. For many years, the project even seemed to be doomed to failure. Eventually, it was pressure brought to bear upon the two antagonistic blocs by Third World countries which secured the approval of the two covenants on 16 December 1966. (Tomuschat 2010)

The International Convention on Civil and Political Rights (ICCPR) and the International Covenant on Economic, Social, and Cultural Rights (ICESCR) were passed unanimously in one resolution (UN Resolution A/RES/2200/A-C[XXI]). The resolution included an optional protocol to the ICCPR to create a mechanism for receiving and investigating complaints about human rights abuses. A second optional protocol was added to the ICCPR in 1989 prohibiting the death penalty (UN Resolution A/RES/44/128). The international community was skeptical that enough states would sign and ratify the ICESCR and the ICCPR. However, the ICESCR received sufficient ratifications and accessions to enter into force in January, 1976, and the ICCPR entered into force in March, 1976.

President Jimmy Carter signed the ICCPR and ICESCR for the United States on October 5, 1977. The U.S. Senate ratified the ICCPR on June 8, 1992, but had not ratified the ICESCR as of the publication of this book. In response to the ratification of the ICCPR, then former President Jimmy Carter stated, "Because of this historic action, the US removes its name from the list of pariah countries, such as China, Saudi Arabia, and South Africa, that have refused to accede to international human rights instruments" (Carter 1992). In a sweeping review of the debate about the role of human rights in U.S. foreign policy, the historian Arthur Schlesinger notes that "Americans have agreed since 1776 that the United States must be the beacon of human rights to an unregenerate world. The question has always been how America is to execute this mission" (Schlesinger 1978, 505). He goes on to review two hundred years of diplomatic history where the United States forged its identity, or at least its image, as a defender of human rights. Why, then, did the United States take so long to sign and ratify the ICCPR and why did it look the other way when its political allies denied human rights? As Schlesinger succinctly stated, "The idea of human rights, like nearly everything else, was caught up in the Cold War" (Schlesinger 1978, 511).

The early 1950s saw the increasing tension of the Cold War and the U.S. identity taking shape as the leader of the Western Bloc in both economic and political affairs. That period also saw a rising tide of isolationism in the U.S. Congress fed by a fear of increasing reliance on multilateral institutions and instruments that both created cooperation (e.g., The UN and the Universal Declaration) and more sharply defined East-West conflict (e.g., NATO and the Warsaw Pact).

On January 7, 1953, John W. Bricker, senator from Ohio, introduced a resolution that was known as the Bricker Amendment. Although there were many versions of the amendment the focus of the effort was to limit presidential power to commit the United States to terms of a treaty that might violate the spirit or the letter of the U.S. Constitution. The amendment would make all treaties non-self-executing. That is, treaties could have no force of law within the United States unless both houses of Congress passed legislation that explicitly enacted the terms of the treaty. The Bricker Amendment arose, in part, out of concerns expressed by the American Bar Association (ABA). The ABA and its president, Frank Holman, reacted to a U.S. Supreme Court case, *Missouri vs. Holland*, in which the Court ruled that a treaty provision could regulate migratory bird hunting even though a law to do so in the absence of the treaty would be a violation of the Tenth Amendment that reserved such regulatory powers to the states (Tananbaum 1985, 75–76). Holman and the ABA were particularly concerned about what this ruling could mean about the human rights provisions in the UN Charter and multilateral conventions on human rights such as the UN Convention on the Prevention of the Crime of Genocide and the ICCPR and the ICESCR. Although Bricker and his ABA supporters couched the amendment in terms of the legal concerns over executive power, it was clearly aimed at preventing the United States from implementing human rights conventions. Arthur Dean noted at the time that although Secretary of State Dulles estimated that around ten thousand executive agreements had been executed in the early years of NATO, supporters of the Bricker Amendment did not target these agreements.

> However, the treaties and other international agreements which have been or are being drafted by the United Nations or its specialized agencies, particularly the Human Rights Covenant and the draft statute for an international criminal court, have been those which the proponents of the amendments have cited as the most convincing examples of the necessity of constitutional protection against international agreements which deny or abridge the fundamental rights of American citizens or interfere in matters that are regarded as essentially local in character. (Dean 1953, 5)

To drive this point home, Senator Bricker declared, "My purpose in offering this resolution is to bury the so-called Covenant on Human Rights so deep that no one holding high public office will ever dare to attempt its resurrection" (U.S. Senate 1952, 8263). President Eisenhower was in sympathy with the intent of the Bricker Amendment but lobbied against it due to its implication for limiting executive power. The amendment failed in the Senate by one vote. However, to get support to defeat the amendment, Eisenhower had to agree that the United States would not accede to any current or future international human rights covenants (Henkin 1995, 348–349).

Eisenhower's promise fit the emerging narrative of the Cold War. The United States would appear to be the champion of universal human rights while supporting the regimes of gross human rights violators such as Anastasio Somoza Debayle in Nicaragua, Augusto Pinochet in Chile, and Ngo Dinh Diem of Vietnam, as long as they supported U.S. backed anti-Soviet policies. In fact, supporting true human rights protections would have been counterproductive to the U.S. foreign policy goals because it would have weakened the ability of leaders such as these to control potentially pro-Soviet reform movements in their countries. Qian and Yanagizawa (2009) showed that the U.S. Department of State based its annual reviews of countries' human rights violations on the country's strategic importance to the United States. They compared the U.S. State Department human rights reports from 112 countries with reports from Amnesty International between 1976 and 2005. The Amnesty International and State Department reports on *non-allies* of the United States were similar throughout the period of the study. For *allies* of the United States, the State Department reports were more favorable than the Amnesty International reports during the Cold War but converged to being similar to the Amnesty International reports after the Cold War was over (Qian and Yanagizawa 2009, 448). Despite Eleanor Roosevelt's call for universal human rights, the United States did not view protection of human rights as a good. As the Cold War progressed, U.S. preferences shifted from the privileged preference ordering for a public good to, at times, perceiving international human rights conventions as public bads.

The individual decision to participate in a human rights regime, like any global public good, depends on the agent's utility for the good. Unlike other global public goods, human rights regimes rest on the creation and dissemination of global norms rather than specific monetary policies or security actions. The discussion about the consensus-building associated with the Universal Declaration shows that norms are constructed in a social environment where the decisions of one agent may affect the willingness to participate in providing the good by other agents. The bandwagon dynamics illustrated in figure 7.1 can create a norm cascade in the life-cycle of norm development. Alternatively, the norm that may be promoted and followed by many agents in a society can be perceived as a pubic bad, rather than a public good, by individual agents. This is often due more to issue linkage than to outright opposition to the substance of the norm. One would hope that the United States was not fundamentally opposed to human rights protection. It did, however, place a higher priority on other Cold War related political objectives and even seemed to believe that human rights regimes interfered with those objectives.

NOTE

1. The abstentions were by Byelorussia, Czechoslovakia, Poland, Saudi Arabia, South Africa, Ukrainian, USSR, and Yugoslavia. The two no-votes were by Honduras and Yemen. A no-vote is not a vote against the resolution. It is, instead, a failure to vote or to abstain formally.

EIGHT

Identities, Utilities, and Public Goods Decisions

THE "PRESUMED" EPISTEMOLOGY
OF RATIONAL CHOICE THEORY

Rational choice theory, as it is practiced, is rooted in a classical empiricist epistemology based on a methodological individualist ontology.[1] Classical empiricism has long been the dominant epistemology in the natural sciences and remains a major approach to inquiry in the social sciences in the face of persistent critique. Promoted by Bacon and Hume, classical empiricism generates knowledge solely through observing the conjunction of atomistic events (Bhaskar 1975, 24). The ultimate goal of science is prediction. Through the symmetry thesis, prediction and explanation are the same thing (Hindmoor 2006, 203; Ruben 1990, 124). Explanation begins with assumptions that are accepted as fact without need for proof. Propositions and theses assert explanations of actors' behaviors *as if* the assumptions are true. Verification of the propositions and theses is achieved by testing falsifiable hypotheses against observable phenomena.

Methodological individualism asserts that individual agents are autonomous agents that make decisions solely based on their own characteristics and properties and that aggregate social phenomena result directly from the collective actions of these autonomous agents. Methodological individualism rejects the possibility that individual agents' actions are due to social structures and it rejects the idea that social structures exist separate from the actions of individual agents.

By embracing classical empiricism and its individualist roots, rational choice theorists explain agents' behavior only in terms of observable phenomena that are external to the agents themselves. Rational choice theory, as practiced, derives its explanations from the observable experiences of individuals. The rationality principle, that actors act to maximize their benefits, is accepted as a nomological law without any attempt at, or need for, explanation. Unobservable factors, such as social structures

121

or psychological characteristics, are excluded from the explanation. Observations are thought to be "objective" because the phenomena of study are themselves treated as objects separate from the observer. The fiction in all of this is that the nomological rationality principle is based on an individual's utility that is an unobserved and unexplained causal factor of choice.

Classical empiricism cannot address or even tolerate unobserved causal factors. Rational choice theory handles this by simply ignoring the source of utilities or, worse, by tautologically defining them in terms of their effects through revealed preference theory. The approach used in this book is different. Yes, utilities are still unobserved or unobservable, but they can be theorized. By taking a constructivist approach to rational choice, this analysis proposes that utilities are derived from the agent's socially constructed identities. Although unobserved, the utilities can be interpreted by examining the social situation of choice. They can then be modeled to determine the effect of the agent's utilities on its preferences for different outcomes of the public goods decision.

THE UTILITY-BASED MODEL OF THE INDIVIDUAL'S PUBLIC GOODS DECISION—A SUMMARY

Given reasonable assumptions about utilities, there are only four possible preference orderings for the 2 x 2 public goods game.[2] The four preference orderings are derived from material threshold conditions along the continuum of decreasing value placed on the public good relative to its costs. This continuum is represented in the decreasing absolute values of the slopes of the indifference curves in each subsequent utility-based model moving from the special privileged model (figure 3.2) to the privileged (figure 3.3) to the intermediate (figure 3.4) and finally to the latent model (figure 3.5). The four preference orderings are determined by material threshold points along the continuum.

The utility-based model of the individual's decision to provide a public good is a two-step process. First, the social construction of the individual's identity in the public goods situation is examined to interpret where the individual's utility for the public good lies on the continuum of value. Second, the resulting preference ordering is used to examine the individual's interactions with other members of the collective to understand the individual's choice and to understand possible public goods outcomes.

Models are generative. They are not predictive. They structure and constrain our thinking to force us to be precise. The result of a model is not an answer. Rather, it is a sense of possibility. Models tell us what is possible when the conditions of the model obtain. A model is not a theory. That is, models are not explanations. Instead, models identify situations that demand theorizing. Models expose elements of our thinking that align with a theory as well as elements that do not. Models never confirm theory. They are too tautological for that. By definition, a model is a representation. It is impossible to represent something without a notion of what that something is. A model is an artifact that replicates our perception of the thing. As such, the model is incapable of discovery. We do not gain knowledge from a model. The model is merely a way of organizing our thinking.

The utility-based models of the public goods decision provide insight into the individual agent's decision whether or not to contribute to global public goods. The United States faced a dilemma in the period after World War II. Its productive capacity was running at record levels, due to the increased production of the war effort. The U.S. gross domestic product growth rate hit 18.9 percent in 1942 (BEA 2019). While the U.S. economy boomed, the rest of the industrialized world suffered from the devastation of the war. The United States was willing and able to provide material and hegemonic leadership in the global economy. The material leadership came first in support of the Bretton Woods institutions and later in the form of the Marshall Plan and other policies to maintain the price of gold and pump dollars into overseas markets. The hegemonic leadership was expressed as a sometimes-imperialist promotion of an open, capitalist, international economy. This willingness to provide leadership waned as the industrialized economies recovered—first with the 1960 gold crisis and finally with the withdrawal of the open gold regime in 1971. By tracking changes in the identities of the United States and the other states through this period, the utility-based models illustrated the decisions to provide the global public good of monetary management.

NATO members found it easy to reach consensus about NATO's primary mission during the Cold War. It was us versus them. NATO was constructed as a clear "us" and the Soviet Union was constructed as a clear "them." Identities were understood and certain. In the post-Cold War world, not only does NATO face an amorphous opponent (al Qaeda, Taliban, ISIS, etc.), but NATO's own identity is unclear. What is the purpose of the alliance? What are its goals? Whom does it protect?

Canada and Greece were caught up in NATO's identity struggles during the Kosovo campaign. Both states were engaged, supportive members of NATO. Canada was one of the original members and Greece began its membership in 1952. Greece and Canada made distinctly different decisions about providing resources to NATO's Kosovo campaign because Greece and Canada had distinctly different identities and interests in that situation of choice. Canada had worked hard over the years to establish itself as a middle power, partly through its participation in peacekeeping missions. Greece was caught between its identity as a member of NATO and the broader European society and its identity as a leader for stability and independence of the Balkan states. Canada's identity led it toward utilities for the collective security regime in Kosovo like those depicted in the privileged utility model. It willingly provided resources for the Kosovo campaign second only to those provided by the United States. Greece's utilities for collective security in Kosovo aligned more with those depicted in the latent utility model. While Greece did not oppose NATO's Kosovo campaign, it also did not provide any material support. In both of these cases, the utility-based models of public goods illustrated the relationship between identity, utility, preferences and the decision whether or not to provide support for the public good.

The evolution of a universal human rights regime took many turns since the end of World War II. In reaction to the horrors of the Holocaust and enamored with the idea of collective action, the member-states of the United Nations forged a consensus that outlined universal values about human rights. Implementation of those values became another matter. Support for universal human rights was supplanted by concerns about sovereign rights and bipolar politics. It took twelve years for the two UN conventions that were meant to implement the Universal Declaration to receive enough ratifications to come into force. The United States only ratified the ICCPR in 1996 and has not yet ratified the ICESCR.

Nevertheless, hope for a universal human rights regime improved at the turn of the twenty-first century with the introduction of the Responsibility to Protect as an emerging norm in international relations. R2P has, perhaps, reached its tipping point and is now cascading through the international system. Once again, acceptance of the norm as an ideal is easier than its implementation. At present, R2P seems to be, at most, a guide for discussion about where to support efforts to stop widespread human rights abuses and, at worst, a justification for intervention by the major powers into the affairs of less powerful states.

The utility-based models provided some insight into this spotty history of universal human rights. The models illustrated the process of consensus-building that occurred in the negotiations over the Universal Declaration of Human Rights. They demonstrated the effect of identity shifts as states acquire and then instantiate the emerging norm of the Responsibility to Protect as it moves through the norm life-cycle. The models also showed what happens when a state, like the United States, views a human rights covenant, like the ICCPR, as a public bad rather than a public good due to its linkage with Cold War politics.

CONCLUSION

Russell Hardin (1971, 474) stated that in the public goods decision, "the dynamic under which Individual performs is clearly the same as that for the Prisoner's Dilemma: his strategy of not paying dominates his strategy of paying." If constructivism in international relations has taught anything, it is that matters of social relations are never pre-determined and fixed. They are always the result of a complex set of social phenomena that includes norms, identities, rules, structures, culture, politics, and history. In the gray nexus between rational choice and constructivism, preferences motivate action, but unlike the hard, exogenous preferences of rational choice theory, constructivist approaches assert that preferences themselves are social constructions. Preferences are always comparisons of utilities. So, this raises the question of how utilities are formed. I do not deny that individuals have unique tastes (after all, I still do not like liver!). Utilities are a synthesis of the individual's idiosyncratic tastes and socially constructed wants and desires. These two dimensions of utility are not uncorrelated, but it is the social dimension of utility that drives the preferences for providing global public goods. Constructivist theories claim that the social dimension of utility derives from rules, social interaction, and norms that identify both the identities that agents can take on and the options that are appropriate for each identity within different social situations of choice.

The utility-based models that are presented in this analysis provide some insights into this process. First, they show that there really are only a small number of preference orderings that make sense when modeling the public goods decision. Second, the four models show that preferences for the public goods result from a continuum of utility relationships from the latent utility model to the special privileged utility model. The preference orderings themselves are mere artifacts of threshold relationships along that continuum. The models are neither determinate nor predictive. They are merely illustrative. They shed a dim light on the unobserved causal factor that has always been responsible for rational choice—the agent's utilities. But since these utilities cannot be observed, their effect must be interpreted in the social relations of the agents and brought to light in the models.

NOTES

1. There are many variants of classical empiricism and many names by which it is known. My usage follows Bhaskar (1975) but other names include instrumental empiricism (MacDonald 2003) and neopositivism (Jackson 2011). Some authors simply refer to it as positivism, but positivism is an ontological position that includes classical empiricism and also includes other epistemologies such as scientific realism that are not directly related to classical empiricism.

2. The "reasonable assumptions" about utility in this model merely state that the individual can aggregate values of different things (the public good and the private good numeraire) into some sort of sense of the total value expected from an outcome.

BIBLIOGRAPHY

Abouharb, M. Rodwan and David L. Cingranelli. 2006. "Human Rights Effects of World Bank Structural Adjustment, 1981–2000." *International Studies Quarterly* 50 (2): 233–263.

Adler, Emmanuel. 1997. "Seizing the Middle Ground: Constructivism in World Politics." *European Journal of International Relations* 3 (3): 319–363.

Aggarwal, Vinod and Cédric Dupont. 1999. "Goods, Games, and Institutions." *International Political Science Review* 20 (4): 393–409.

———. 2002. "Goods, Games, and Institutions: A Reply." *International Political Science Review* 23 (4): 402–410.

———. 2003. "Comment on 'Common Goods, Matrix Games, and Institutional Response' by Katharina Holzinger." *European Journal of International Relations* 9 (3): 475–478.

Ahn, T. K., Elinor Ostrom, and James M. Walker. 2003. "Heterogeneous Preferences and Collective Action." *Public Choice* 117 (3/4): 295–314.

Ahn, T. K., Elinor Ostrom, David Schmidt, Robert Shupp, and James Walker 2001. "Cooperation in PD Games: Fear, Greed, and History of Play." *Public Choice* 106 (1/2): 137–155.

American Anthropological Association. 1947. "Statement on Human Rights." *American Anthropologist* 49 (4): 539–543.

Andreoni, James. 1988. "Privately Provided Public Goods in a Large Economy: The Limits of Altruism." *Journal of Public Economics* 35 (1): 57–73.

———. 1990. "Impure Altruism and Donations to Public Goods: A Theory of Warm-Glow Giving." *The Economic Journal* 100 (401): 464–477.

———. 1995. "Cooperation in Public-Goods Experiments: Kindness or Confusion?" *The American Economic Review* 85 (4): 891–904.

Annan, Kofi. 1999. "Secretary-General Presents His Annual Report to General Assembly." United Nations General Assembly, Press Release SG/SM/7136, 20 September 1999. Retrieved from https://www.un.org/press/en/1999/19990920.sgsm7136.html on November 4, 2018.

———. 2000. *'We the Peoples': The Role of the United Nations in the 21st Century*. New York: United Nations Department of Public Information.

Apple, R. W., Jr. 1999. "A Fresh Set of U.S. Goals." *ProQuest Historical Newspapers: The New York Times with Index*. March 25, 1999. Retrieved from www.proquest.com/products-services/pq-hist-news.html on February 19, 2018.

———. 1996. "Why Western Europe Needs the United States and NATO." *Political Science Quarterly* 111 (1): 1–39.

Art, Robert J. 1980. "To What Ends Military Power?" *International Security* 4 (4): 3–35.

Archetti, Marco and István Scheuring. 2012. "Game Theory of Public Goods in One-Shot Social Dilemmas Without Assortment." *Journal of Theoretical Biology* 299: 9–20.

Ashley, Richard. 1987. "Foreign Policy as Political Performance." *International Studies Notes* 13 (2): 51–55.

Associated Press. 1999. "Greece Calls for Kosovo Truce." *Associated Press Newswire*, April 5, 1999. Retrieved from *Factiva*, https://www.dowjones.com/products/factiva/ on February 24, 2018.

Austen-Smith, David. 1980. "Individual Contribution to Public Goods." *Economic Letters* 5: 359–361.

Axelrod, Robert. 1980. "Effective Choice in the Prisoner's Dilemma." *Journal of Conflict Resolution* 24 (1): 3–25.

———. 1981. "The Emergence of Cooperation among Egoists." *American Political Science Review* 75 (2): 306–318.

———. 1984. *The Evolution of Cooperation*. New York: Basic Books.

Barrett, Scott. 2007. *Why Cooperate? The Incentive to Supply Global Public Goods*. New York: Oxford University Press.

Bashow, David L., Dwight Davies, Andre Viens, John Rotteau, Norman Balfe, Ray Stouffer, James Pickett, and Steve Harris. 2000. "Mission Ready: Canada's Role in the Kosovo Air Campaign." *Canadian Military Journal* (Spring): 55–61.

BBC. 2018. "Greece Macedonia: Name Dispute Draws Mass Protest in Athens." *BBC Online*. Retrieved from http://www.bbc.com/news/world-europe-42937889 on February 24, 2018.

Becker, Gary S. 1986. "The Economic Approach to Human Behavior." In *Rational Choice* edited by Jon Elster, 108–122. New York: New York University Press.

———. 1996. *Accounting for Tastes*. Cambridge, Mass.: Harvard University Press.

Beitz, Charles R. 2009. *Introduction to the Idea of Human Rights*. Oxford: Oxford University Press.

Bieler, Andreas and Adam David Morton. 2004. "A Critical Theory Route to Hegemony, World Order and Historical Change." *Capital & Class* 28 (1): 85–113.

Bellamy, Alex J. 2010. "The Responsibility to Protect—5 Years On." *Ethics and International Affairs* 24 (2): 143–169.

Bentham, Jeremy. 1823. *An Introduction to the Principles of Morals and Legislation*. London: Clarendon Press. Reproduced online by the Online Library of Liberty. Retrieved from http://oll.libertyfund.org/sources/1202-facsimile-PDF-bentham- an-introduction-to- the-principles-of-morals-and-legislation/download/ on October 2, 2017.

———. 2011. *Selected Writings*. Edited by Stephen G. Engelmann. New Haven: Yale University Press.

Berger, Peter. 1966. "Identity as a Problem in the Sociology of Knowledge." *European Journal of Sociology* 7 (1): 32–40.

Bergstrom, Theodore, Lawrence Blume, and Hal Varian. 1986. "On the Private Provision of Public Goods." *Journal of Public Economics* 29 (1): 25–49.

Bhaskar, Roy. 1975. *A Realist Theory of Science.* New York: Verso.

Blackden, Richard. 2011. "History of Bretton Woods." *The Telegraph* April 9, 2011. Retrieved from http://www.telegraph.co.uk/finance/economics/8439898/History-of-Bretton-Woods.html on December 19, 2017.

Bliss, Christopher and Barry Nalebuff. 1984. "Dragon Slaying and Ballroom Dancing: The Private Supply of a Public Good." *Journal of Public Economics* 25 (1/2): 1–12.

Bobango, Gerald J. 1979. *The Emergence of the Romanian National State.* Boulder, Colo.: East European Quarterly. Distributed by Columbia University Press, New York.

Boia, Eugene. 1993. *Romania's Diplomatic Relations with Yugoslavia in the Interwar Period, 1919–1941.* Boulder, Colo.: East European Monographs. Distributed by Columbia University Press, New York.

Brams, Steven. 1994. *Theory of Moves.* Cambridge: Cambridge University Press.

Brams, Steven J. and Walter Mattli. 1993. "Theory of Moves: Overview and Examples." *Conflict Management and Peace Science* 12 (2): 1–39.

Brown, Keith and Dimitrios Theodossopoulos. 2003. "Rearranging Solidarity: Conspiracy and World Order in Greek and Macedonian Commentaries on Kosovo." *Journal of Southern Europe and the Balkans* 5 (3): 315–335.

Brubaker, Rogers and Frederick Cooper. 2000. "Beyond Identity." *Theory and Society* 29 (1): 1–47.

Buchanan, James. 1968. *The Demand and Supply of Public Goods.* New York: Rand McNally and Company.

Bureau of Economic Analysis (BEA). 2019. "National Income and Product Account Tables: Table 1.1.1 GDP Growth Rate." U.S. Department of Commerce.

Campbell, David. 1998. *Writing Security: United States Foreign Policy and the Politics of Identity.* Revised edition. Minneapolis, Minn.: University of Minnesota Press.

Canada History. 2013. "Peacekeeping." Retrieved from http://www.canadahistory.com/sections/war/Peace%20Keepers/peacekeeping.html on March 26, 2017.

Carter, Charles and David M. Malone. 2016. "The Origins and Evolution of Responsibility to Protect at the UN." *International Relations* 30 (3): 278–297.

Carter, Jimmy. 1992. "US Finally Ratifies Human Rights Covenant." *The Christian Science Monitor* June 29, 1992.

Central Intelligence Agency (CIA). 2017. "Serbia." *The World Factbook.* Retrieved from https://www.cia.gov/library/publications/the-world-factbook/geos/ri.html on March 24, 2017.

Cernicova-Buca, Mariana. 2001. "Romania: The Quest for Membership." In *Enlarging NATO: The National Debates,* edited by Gale A. Mattox and Arthur R. Rachwald, 199–217. Boulder, Colo.: Lynne Rienner Publishers.

Charnysh, Volha, Paulette Lloyd, and Beth A. Simmons. 2015. "Frames and consensus formation in international relations: The case of trafficking in persons." *European Journal of International Relations* 21 (2): 323–351.

Chiang, Alpha C. 1974. *Fundamental Methods of Mathematical Economics.* Second edition. New York: McGraw Hill.

Chong, Dennis and James N. Druckman. 2007. "A Theory of Framing and Opinion Formation in Competitive Elite Environments." *Journal of Communication* 57 (1): 99–118.

Cialdini, Robert R. 2001. "Harnessing the Science of Persuasion." *Harvard Business Review* 79 (9) (October): 72–79.

———. 2008. *Influence: Science and Practice.* Fifth edition. New York: Allyn and Bacon.

Clarke, Kevin A. and David M. Primo. 2007. "Modernizing Political Science: A Model-Based Approach." *Perspectives on Politics* 5 (4): 741–753.

Clinton, William J. 1996. "Transcript of the Remarks by President W. J. Clinton To People of Detroit, October 22, 1996." *NATO Transcript of Speeches 1996.* Retrieved from https://www.nato.int/docu/speech/1996/s961022a.htm on February 12, 2018.

Cohen, Benjamin J. 1977. *Organizing the World's Money: The Political Economy of International Monetary Relations.* New York: Basic Books.

Conybeare, John. 1984. "Public Goods, Prisoner's Dilemmas, and the International Political Economy." *International Studies Quarterly* 28 (1): 5–22.

Cooley, Jason. 2006. "The War on Terrorism and the Need for Altercasting." *Defense and Security Analysis* 22 (3): 315–323.

Cornes, Richard and Todd Sandler. 1996. *The Theory of Externalities, Public Goods, and Club Goods.* Second edition. Cambridge: Cambridge University Press.

Cox, Robert W. 1992. "Towards a Posthegemonic Conceptualization of World Order: Reflections on the Relevancy of Ibn Khaldun." In *Approaches to World Order,* edited by Robert W. Cox and Timothy J. Sinclair. Cambridge: Cambridge University Press.

Crider, John H. 1944a. "Ten Billion Total Seen for Exports." *ProQuest Historical Newspapers: The New York Times with Index,* July 4, 1944. Retrieved from www.proquest.com/products-services/pq-hist-news.html on February 26, 2016.

———. 1944b. Peruvians Demand World Trade Plan. *ProQuest Historical Newspapers: The New York Times with Index,* July 18, 1944. Retrieved from www.proquest.com/products-services/pq-hist-news.html on February 26, 2016.

Davidson, Donald. 1963. "Actions, Reasons, and Causes." *The Journal of Philosophy* 60 (23): 585–700.

De Felice, Damiano and Francesco Obino. 2012. "Editors' Introduction: Weaving the Theories of Practice and International Relations." *Millennium: Journal of International Relations* 40 (3): 431–437.

De Moor, Tine. 2015. *The Dilemma of the Commoners: Understanding the Use of Common Pool Resources in Long-Term Perspective.* New York: Cambridge University Press.

Dean, Arthur H. 1953. "The Bricker Amendment and Authority over Foreign Affairs." *Foreign Affairs* 32 (1): 1–19.

Deng, Francis, Sadikiel Kimaro, Terrence Lyons, Donald Rothchild, and I. William Zartman. 1996. *Sovereignty as Responsibility: Conflict Management in Africa.* Washington, D.C.: The Brookings Institution.

Donnelly, Jack. 2003. *Universal Human Rights in Theory and Practice.* Second edition. Ithaca: Cornell University Press.

———. 2013. *Universal Human Rights in Theory and Practice.* Third edition. Ithaca: Cornell University Press.

Dow Jones. 1999. "Romanian President Favors Letting NATO Use Airspace." *Dow Jones Newswires.* Retrieved from *Factiva,* https://global-factiva-com on January 5, 2019.

Druckman, James N. and Arthur Lupia. 2000. "Preference Formation." *Annual Review of Political Science* 3: 1–24.

Eichengreen, Barry. 2011. *Exorbitant Privilege: The Rise and Fall of the Dollar and the Future of the International Monetary System*. New York: Oxford University Press.

Engerer, Hella. 2011. "Security as a Public, Private or Club Good: Some Fundamental Considerations." *Defence and Peace Economics* 22 (2): 135–145.

Erikson, Erik H. 1950. *Childhood and Society*. New York: W. W. Norton and Company.

———. 1968. *Identity: Youth and Crisis*. New York: W. W. Norton and Company.

Erlanger, Steven. 1998. "Albright Warns Serbs on Violence." *ProQuest Historical Newspapers: The New York Times with Index*. March 8, 1998. Retreived from www. proquest.com/products-services/pq-hist-news.html on April 6, 2019.

Esteban, Joan and Debraj Ray. 2001. "Collective Action and the Group-Size Paradox." *American Political Science Review* 95 (3): 663–672.

Etzioni, Amitai. 2006. "Sovereignty as Responsibility." *Orbis* 50 (1): 71–85.

European Union. 1992. "Treaty on European Union (Maastricht Treaty)." Retrieved from https://europa.eu/european-union/sites/europaeu/files/docs/body/ treaty_on_european_ union_en.pdf on January 5, 2019.

———. 2000. Charter of Fundamental Rights of the European Union. *Official Journal of the European Communities*. Document ID: 2000/C 364.

Evans, Gareth, et al. 2001. *The Responsibility to Protect. Report of the International Commission on Intervention and State Sovereignty*. Ottawa: International Development Research Center.

Everts, Philip. 2003. "War without Bloodshed? Public Opinion and the Conflict over Kosovo." In *Public Opinion and the International Use of Force*, edited by Philip Everts and Pierangelo Isernia Kindle edition. New York: Routledge.

Faure, Michael, Peter Mascini, and Jing Liu. 2017. *Environmental Governance and Common Pool Resources*. London: Routledge.

Fehr, Ernst and Klaus M. Schmidt. 1999. "A Theory of Fairness and Cooperation." *The Quarterly Journal of Economics* 114 (3): 817–868.

Ferejohn, John. 1991. "Rationality and Interpretation: Parliamentary Elections in Early Stuart England." In *The Economic Approach to Politics*, edited by Kristen Renwick Monroe, 279–305. New York: Harper Collins.

Fershtman, Chaim and Shmuel Nitzan. 1991. "Dynamic Voluntary Provision of Public Goods." *European Economic Review* 35: 1057–1067.

Finnemore, Martha. 1996. *National Interests in International Society*. Ithaca: Cornell University Press.

Finnemore, Martha and Kathryn Sikkink. 1998. "International Norm Dynamics and Political Change." *International Organization* 52 (4): 887–917.

Fogarty, T. M. 1981. "Prisoner's Dilemmas and Other Public Goods Games." *Conflict Management and Peace Science* 5: 111–120.

Forsythe, David P. 1998. "Human Rights Fifty Years after the Universal Declaration." *PS: Political Science and Politics* 31 (3): 505–511.

Fowler, James H. and Henry C. Harpending. 2005. "Altruistic Punishment and the Origin of Cooperation." *Proceedings of the National Academy of Sciences of the United States of America* 102(19): 7047–7049.

Freeman, Michael. 1994. "The Philosophical Foundations of Human Rights." *Human Rights Quarterly* 16: 491–514.

Friedman, Milton. 2008 [1962]. *Price Theory, with a New Introduction by Steven Medema*. New Brunswick, N.J.: AldineTransaction.

Frohlich, Norman, Thomas Hunt, Joe Oppenheimer, and R. Harrison Wagner. 1975. "Individual Contributions for Collective Goods: Alternative Models." *The Journal of Conflict Resolution* 19 (2): 310–329.

Frohlich, Norman and Joe A. Oppenheimer. 1970. "I Get by with a Little Help from My Friends." *World Politics* 23 (1): 104–120.

Giddens, Anthony. 1984. *The Constitution of Society: Outline of a Theory of Sturcturation*. Berkeley: University of California Press.

Gillespie, Mark. 1999. "Crisis in Kosovo: Questions and Answers About American Public Opinion." *Gallup News Service*. Retrieved from http://news.gallup.com/poll/3925/crisis-kosovo-questions-answers-about-american-public-opinion.aspx on February 3, 2018.

Gilpin, Robert. 1987. *The Political Economy of International Relations*. Princeton, N.J.: Princeton University Press.

———. 2001. *Global Political Economy: Understanding the International Economic Order*. Princeton, N.J.: Princeton University Press.

Glanville, Luke. 2014. *Sovereignty and the Responsibility to Protect: A New History*. Chicago: University of Chicago Press.

———. 2016. "Does R2P Matter? Interpreting the Impact of a Norm." *Cooperation and Conflict* 51 (2): 184–199.

Glendon, Mary Ann. 2001. *A World Made New: Eleanor Roosevelt and the Declaration of Human Rights*. New York: Random House.

Glimcher, Paul W., Michael C. Dorris, and Hannah M. Bayer. 2005. "Physiological Utility Theory and the Neuroeconomics of Choice." *Games and Economic Behavior* 52: 213–256.

Granatstein, Jack L. 1993. "Canada and Peacekeeping: Image and Reality." In *Canadian Foreign Policy: Historical Readings*, edited by Jack L. Granatstein, 232–240. Toronto: Copp Clark Pitman Ltd.

Griffin, James. 2008. *On Human Rights*. New York: Oxford University Press.

Hafner-Burton, Emilie M., Kiyoteru Tsutsui, and John W. Meyer. 2008. "International Human Rights Law and the Politics of Legitimation: Repressive States and Human Rights Treaties." *International Sociology* 23 (1): 115–141.

Haglund, David G. and Allen Sens. 2000. "Kosovo and the Case of the (Not So) Free Riders: Portugal, Belgium, Canada, and Spain." In *Kosovo and the Challenge of Humanitarian Intervention: Selective Indignation, Collective Action, and International Citizenship*, edited by Albrecht Schnabel and Ramesh Thakur, 181–200. New York: United Nations University Press.

Hardin, Russell. 1971. "Collective Action as an Agreeable n-Prisoner's Dilemma." *Behavioral Science* 16: 472–481.

———. 1982. *Collective Action*. Baltimore: Johns Hopkins University Press.

Hartzell, Caroline A., Matthew Hoddie, and Molly Bauer. 2010. "Economic Liberalization via IMF Structural Adjustment: Sowing the Seeds of Civil War?" *International Organization* 64 (2): 339–356.

Haug, Christoph. 2015. "What is Consensus and How Is It Achieved in Meetings?" In *The Cambridge Handbook of Meeting Science*, edited by Joseph A. Allen and Nale Lehmann-Willenbrock, 556–584. New York: Cambridge University Press.

Heap, Shaun H., Martin Hollis, Bruce Lyons, Robert Sugden, and Albert Weal. 1992. *The Theory of Choice: A Critical Guide*. Oxford, U.K.: Blackwell Publishers Ltd.

Hechter, Michael. 1992. "The Insufficiency of Game Theory for the Resolution of Real-World Collective Action Problems." *Rationality and Society* 14 (1): 33–40.

Heckathorn, Douglas, D. 1996. "The Dynamics and Dilemmas of Collective Action." *American Sociological Review* 61 (2): 250–277.

Helleiner, Eric. 1994. *States and the Reemergence of Global Finance: From Bretton Woods to the 1990s*. Ithaca, NY: Cornell University Press.

Henkin, Louis. 1995. "U.S. Ratification of Human Rights Conventions: The Ghost of Senator Bricker." *American Journal of International Law* 89 (2): 341–350.

———.1999. "Kosovo and the Law of 'Humanitarian Intervention.'" *American Journal of International Law* 93 (4): 824–828.

Herring, Hubert B. 1998. "June 7–13: NATO Warns Serbs." *New York Times*, Online Archives, http://www.nytimes.com/1998/06/14/weekinreview/june-7-13-nato-warns-serbs.html?scp=25&sq=kosovo&st=nyt. Accessed on February 14, 2010.

Higgins, Tracy E. 1996. "Anti-Essentialism, Relativism, and Human Rights." *Harvard Women's Law Journal* 19: 89–126.

Hindmoor, Andrew. 2006. *Rational Choice*. New York: Palgrave/Macmillan.

Hirschman, Albert O. 1945. *National Power and the Structure of Foreign Trade*. Berkeley, Calif.: University of California Press.

Hirshleifer, Jack. 1980. *Price Theory and Its Applications*. Second edition. Englewood Cliffs, N.J.: Prentice-Hall.

———. 1983. "From Weakest-Link to Best-Shot: The Voluntary Provision of Public Goods." *Public Choice* 41 (3): 371–386.

———. 1999. "There Are Many Evolutionary Paths to Cooperation." *Journal of Bioeconomics* 1: 73–93.

Hogg, Michael A., Deborah J. Terry, and Katherine M. White. 1995. "A Tale of Two Theories: A Critical Comparison of Identity Theory with Social Identity Theory." *Social Psychology Quarterly* 58 (4): 255–269.

Holbrooke, Richard. 1995. "America, a European Power." *Foreign Affairs* 74 (2): 38–51.

Hollis, Martin. 1987. *The Cunning of Reason*. Cambridge: Cambridge University Press.

Holzinger, Katharina. 2003. "Common Goods, Matrix Games, and Institutional Response." *European Journal of International Relations* 9 (3): 173–212.

Hopf, Ted. 2002. *Social Construction of International Politics: Identities and Foreign Policies, Moscow, 1955 and 1999*. Ithaca, N.Y.: Cornell University Press.

———. 2010. "The Logic of Habit in International Relations." *European Journal of International Relations* 16 (4): 539–561.

Hunt, Lynn. 2007. *Inventing Human Rights: A History*. New York: W.W. Norton and Company.

Hutten, E. F. 1954. "The Rôle of Models in Physics." *The British Journal for the Philosophy of Science* 4 (16): 284–301.

International Monetary Fund (IMF). 1944. "Articles of Agreement." Retrieved from https://fraser.stlouisfed.org/files/docs/historical/martin/17_07_19440701. pdf on January 10, 2019.

———. 2001. "Money Matters: An IMF Exhibit—The Importance of Global Cooperation—Deconstruction and Reconstruction 1945–1958." Retrieved from www .imf.org/external/np/exr/center/mm/eng/mm_dr_01.htm, on February 28, 2016.

Irish Times. 1999. "Majority in Greece Wants Clinton Tried for War Crimes over Kosovo." *The Irish Times,* May 27, 1999: 13. Retrieved from http://www.lexus nexis.com on March 27, 2017.

Jackson, Patrick Thaddeus. 2011. *The Conduct of Inquiry in International Relations: Philosophy of Science and its Implications for the World Politics.* New York: Routledge.

Jevons, William Stanley. 1888. *The Theory of Political Economy.* Third edition. London: Macmillan. Retrieved from http://www.econlib.org/library/YPD Books/ Jevons/jvnPE.html on August 23, 2017.

Kahneman, Daniel and Jackie Snell. 1990. "Predicting Utility." In *Insights in Decision Making, a Tribute to Hillel J. Einhorn,* edited by Robin M. Hogarth, 295–310. Chicago: University of Chicago Press.

Kahneman, Daniel, Peter P. Wakker, and Rakesh Saren. 1997. "Back to Bentham? Explorations of Experienced Utility." *The Quarterly Journal of Economics* 112 (2): 375–405.

Kaptien, Maurits, et al. 2009. "Can You Be Persuaded? Individual Differences in Susceptibility to Persuasion." *Human-Computer Interaction—INTERACT 2009,* Proceedings of the 13th International Federation for Information Processing Conference, Part I. Edited by T. Gross, et al., Upsala, Sweden: 115–118.

Kaul, Inge, Isabelle Grunberg, and Marc Stern, editors. 1999. *Global Public Goods: International Cooperation in the 21st Century.* New York: Oxford University Press.

Kaul, Inge, Pedro Conceição, Katell Le Goulven, and Ronald U. Mendoza, editors. 2003. *Providing Global Public Goods: Managing Globalization.* New York: Oxford University Press.

Kealey, Terrence and Martin Ricketts. 2014. "Modeling Science as a Contribution Good." *Research Policy* 43 (6): 1014–1024.

Keck, Margaret E. and Kathryn Sikkink. 1998. *Activists beyond Borders.* Ithaca, N.Y.: Cornell University Press.

Keefe, Eugene K., Donald Bernier, et al. 1970. *Area Handbook for Romania.* Washington, D.C.: United States Government Printing Office.

Keohane, Robert O. 1980. "The theory of hegemonic stability and changes in international economic regimes, 1967–1977." In *Change in the International System,* edited by Ole Holsti et al., 325–355. Boulder: Westview Press.

———. 1982. "Hegemonic leadership and U.S. foreign economic policy in the Long Decade of the 1950s." In *America in a Changing World Political Economy,* edited by William Avery and David Rapkin, 49–76. New York: Longman.

Kindleberger, Charles. 1973. *The World in Depression 1929-1939,* Berkeley, Calif.: University of California Press.

———. 1981. "Dominance and Leadership in the International Economy." *International Studies Quarterly* 25 (3): 242–254.

Kollock, Peter. 1998. Social Dilemmas: The Anatomy of Cooperation. *Annual Review of Sociology* 24: 183–214.

Kondopoulou, Margarita. 2002. The Greek Media and the Kosovo Crisis. *Conflict & Communication Online* 1 (2): 1–11.

Kowert, Paul A. 1998. "Agent versus Structure in the Construction of National Identity." In *International Relations in a Constructed World,* edited by Vendulka Kubálková, Nicholas G. Onuf, and Paul A. Kowert, 101–122. Armonk, N.Y.: M.E. Sharpe.

———. 2001. "Toward a Constructivist Theory of Foreign Policy." In *Foreign Policy in a Constructed World,* edited by Vendulka Kubálková, 266–287. Armonk, N.Y.: M.E. Sharpe.

Krahmann, Elke. 2008. "Security: Collective Good or Commodity?" *European Journal of International Relations* 14 (3): 379–404.

Krasner, Stephen. 1975. "State Power and the Structure of International Trade." *World Politics* 27 (3): 314–347.

Krieger, Heike. 2001a. *The Kosovo Conflict and International Law: An Analytical Documentation, 1974–1999.* New York: Cambridge University Press.

———. 2001b. "Interim Agreement for Peace and Self-Government in Kosovo, Rambouillett, 23 February 1999." In The *Kosovo Conflict and International Law: An Analytical Documentation, 1974–1999,* edited by Heike Krieger, 261–278. New York: Cambridge University Press.

———. 2001c. "Greece and the New Millennium: Signposts to a Point of Departure, Speech by the Greek Prime Minister Costas Simitis, Woodrow Wilson School, United States, April 1999." In The *Kosovo Conflict and International Law: An Analytical Documentation, 1974–1999,* edited by Heike Krieger, 404–405. New York: Cambridge University Press.

Kritsiotis, Dino. 2000. "The Kosovo Crisis and NATO's Application of Armed Force against the Federal Republic of Yugoslavia." *The International and Comparative Law Quarterly* 49 (2): 330–359.

Krook, Mona L. and Jacqui True. 2012. "Rethinking the Life Cycles of International Norms: The United Nations and the Global Promotion of Gender Equality." *European Journal of International Relations* 18 (1): 103–127.

Kubálková, Vendulka. 2001. "Foreign Policy, International Politics, and Constructivism." In *Foreign Policy in a Constructed World,* edited by Vendulka Kubálková, 15–37. Armonk, N.Y.: M.E. Sharpe.

Kubálková, Vendulka, Nicholas G. Onuf, and Paul A. Kowert. Editors. 1998. *International Relations in a Constructed World.* Armonk, N.Y.: M.E. Sharpe.

Labonte, Melissa. 2016. "R2P's Status as a Norm." In *The Oxford Handbook of the Responsibility to Protect,* edited by Alex J. Bellamy and Tim Dunne, 133–150. New York: Oxford University Press.

Lake, David. A. 1988. *Power, Protection, and Free Trade: The International Sources of American Commercial Strategy, 1887–1939.* Ithaca, N.Y.: Cornell University Press.

Lambeth, Benjamin S. 2001. NATO's *Air War for Kosovo: A Strategic and Operational Assessment.* Kindle online edition. Santa Monica, Calif.: RAND Corporation.

Larrabee, F. Stephen. 2005. "Greece's Balkan Policy in a New Strategic Era." *Southeast European and Black Sea Studies* 5 (3): 405–425.

Lebow, Richard Ned. 2008. "Identity and International Relations." *International Relations* 22: 473–492.

Lialiouti, Zinovia. 2011. "Greek Anti-Americanism and the War in Kosovo." *National Identities* 13 (2): 127–156.

———. 2015. "Greek Cold War Anti-Americanism in Perspective, 1947–1989." *Journal of Transatlantic Studies* 13 (1): 40–55.

Lichbach, M. 1992. "The Repeated Public Goods Game: A Solution Using Tit-for-Tat and the Lindahl Point." *Theory and Decision* 32 (2): 133–146.

Lipnowski, Irwin and Shlomo Maital. 1983. "Voluntary Provision of a Pure Public Good as a Game of Chicken." *Journal of Public Economics* 20 (3): 381–386.

Lomasky, Loren. 1987. *Persons, Rights, and the Moral Community.* New York: Oxford University Press.

Lukes, Stephen. 1994. "Five Fables about Human Rights." *Filozofski Vestnik* 15 (2): 111–126.

MacDonald, Paul K. 2003. "Useful Fiction or Miracle Maker: The Competing Epistemological Foundations of Rational Choice Theory." *American Political Science Review* 97 (4): 551–565.

MacIntyre, Alisdair. 2007. *After Virtue: A Study in Moral Theory.* New York: Bloomsbury Academic.

Maddison, Angus. 2007. *Contours of the World Economy 1–2030 AD: Essays in Macro-Economic History.* Oxford: Oxford University Press.

Makris, Miltiadis. 2009. "Private Provision of Discrete Public Goods." *Games and Economic Behavior* 67 (1): 292–299.

Malita, Mircea. 1970. *Romanian Diplomacy: A Historical Study.* Bucharest: Meridiane Publishing House.

Malle, Bertram F. 1999. "How People Explain Behavior: A New Theoretical Framework." *Personality and Social Psychology Review* 3 (1): 23–48.

Maloney, Sean M. 2005. "From Myth to Reality Check; From Peacekeeping to Stabilization." *Policy Options* September: 40–46.

Manolache, Diana and Ciprian Chis. 2015. NATO Bombing in the Former Republic of Yugoslavia. *Proceedings of the Scientific Conference AFASES* 1: 61–69.

March, James G. and Johan P. Olsen. 1989. *Rediscovering Institutions.* New York: Free Press.

———. 1998. "The Institutional Dynamics of International Political Orders." *International Organization* 52 (4): 943–969.

———. 2004. "The Logic of Appropriateness." ARENA Working Paper WP/04/09, Centre for European Studies, University of Oslo. Retrieved from https://www.sv.uio.no/arena/english/research/publications/arena-publications/work ingpapers/working-papers2004/ wp04_9.pdf, January 30, 2015.

Mason, General Paul D. 1988. "Peacekeeping in a Changing World. Speech to the Empire Club on November 17, 1988." *Canadian Speeches* 2 (8): 35–41.

McKeown, Timothy J. 1983. "Hegemonic Stability Theory and 19th Century Tariff Levels in Europe." *International Organization* 37 (1): 73–91.

———. 1991. "A Liberal Trade Order? The Long-Run Pattern of Imports to the Advanced Capitalist States." *International Studies Quarterly* 35 (2): 151–171.

Mearsheimer, John. 2013. "Structural Realism." In *International Relations Theory: Discipline and Diversity*. Third edition, edited by Tim Dunne et al., 77–93. New York: Oxford University Press.

Medina, Luis F. 2005. "The Comparative Statics of Collective Action: A Pragmatic Approach to Games with Multiple Equilibria." *Rationality and Society* 17 (4): 423–452.

Mendus, Susan. 1995. "Human Rights in Political Theory." *Political Studies* 63: 10–24.

Merriam-Webster. 2018. "Definition of Consensus." Retrieved from https://www.merriam-webster.com/dictionary/consensus on April 23, 2018.

Messari, Nizar. 2001. "Identity and Foreign Policy: The Case of Islam in U.S. Foreign Policy." In *Foreign Policy in a Constructed World*, edited by Vendulka Kubálková. 277–246. Armonk, N.Y.: M.E. Sharpe.

Meyer, John W., John Boli, George M. Thomas, and Francisco M. Ramirez. 1997. "World Society and the Nation-State." *American Journal of Sociology* 103 (1): 144–181.

Michas, Tachis. 2002. *Unholy Alliance*. College Station, Tex.: Texas A&M University Press.

Migdalovitz, Carol. 1999. "Kosovo: Greek and Turkish Perspectives." *CRS Report for Congress*. Washington, D.C.: Congressional Research Service, the Library of Congress.

Morrow, James D. 1994. *Game Theory for Political Scientists*. Princeton, N.J.: Princeton University Press.

Morsink, Johannes. 1999. *The Universal Declaration of Human Rights: Origins, Drafting and Intent*. Philadelphia: University of Pennsylvania Press.

Mueller, Dennis C. 1989. *Public Choice II: A Revised Edition of Public Choice*. Cambridge: Cambridge University Press.

NATO. 1995. *Study on NATO Enlargement*. Accessed at http://www.nato.int/docu/basictxt/enl-9501.htm on January 2, 2005.

———. 1998a. "Statement by the Secretary General following the ACTWARN decision." Press Statement - Vilamoura - 24 Sept. 1998. Retrieved from http://nato.int/docu/pr/1998/p980924e.htm on March 22, 2017.

———. 1998b. "Statement to the Press by the Secretary General Following Decision on the ACTORD." NATO HQ, 13 Oct. 1998. Retrieved from http://nato.int/docu/speech/1998/s981013a.htm on March 26, 2017.

———. 1999a. "Statement by the North Atlantic Council on Kosovo." Press Release (99)12, 30 Jan. 1999. Retrieved from http://nato.int/docu/pr/1999/p99-012e.htm on March 21, 2017.

———. 1999b. "Press Statement by Dr. Javier Solana, Secretary General of NATO." Press Release (1999)040, 23 March 1999. Retrieved from http://nato.int/docu/pr/1999/p99-040e.htm on March 21, 2017.

———. 1999c. "The Accession of the Czech Republic, Hungary and Poland. North Atlantic Treaty Organization Press Release." Retrieved from https://www.nato int/docu/comm/1999/9904-wsh/pres-eng/03acce.pdf on February 25, 2018.

———. 2000a. "Financial and Economic Data Relating to NATO Defence: Defence Expenditures of NATO Countries (1980–2000)." North Atlantic Treaty Organization, Press Release M-DPC-2(2000) 107, issued on 05 Dec. 2000, updated 14 Jun. 2010. Retrieved from https://www.nato.int/cps/en/natolive/news_18156.htm?mode=pressrelease, on February 11, 2018.

———. 2017. "Peace Support Operations in Bosnia and Herzegovina." North Atlantic Treaty Organization. Retrieved from https://www.nato.int/cps/en/natohq/topics_52122.htm? selectedLocale=en on February 25, 2018.

Neumann, Iver B. 2002. "Returning Practice to the Linguistic Turn: The Case of Diplomacy." *Millennium: Journal of International Studies* 31 (3): 627–651.

New York Times. 1944a. "Message of the President." *ProQuest Historical Newspapers: The New York Times with Index,* July 2, 1944. Retrieved from www.proquest.com/products-services/pq-hist-news.html on February 26, 2016.

———. 1944b. "Text of the Articles of Agreement Reached by 44 Countries at the Monetary Parlay." *ProQuest Historical Newspapers: The New York Times with Index,* July 23, 1944. Retrieved from www.proquest.com/products-services/pq-hist-news.html on February 26, 2016.

———. 1960a. "U.S. Asks Bonn Aid in Payment Drain." *ProQuest Historical Newspapers: The New York Times with Index,* November 1, 1960. Retrieved from www.proquest.com/products-services/pq-hist-news.html on February 26, 2016.

———. 1960b. "The Transcript of Eisenhower's News Conference." *ProQuest Historical Newspapers: The New York Times with Index,* November 17, 1960. Retrieved from www.proquest.com/products-services/pq-hist-news.html on June 3, 2018.

Nickel, James W. 2007. *Making Sense of Human Rights.* Second edition. New York: Blackwell.

Nixon, Richard. 1971. "Address to the Nation Outlining a New Economic Policy: 'The Challenge of Peace.' August 15, 1971." Provided online by Gerhard Peters and John T. Woolley, *The American Presidency Project.* Retrieved from https://www.presidency.ucsb.edu/documents/address-the-nation-outlining-new-economic-policy-the-challenge-peace on March 6, 2016.

Nunn, Geoffrey E. and Thayer H. Watkins. 1978. "Public Goods Games." *Southern Economic Journal* 45 (2): 598–606.

Olson, Mancur. 1971 [1965]. *The Logic of Collective Action, Public Goods and the Theory of Groups.* Cambridge, Mass.: Harvard University Press.

Olson, Mancur, Jr. and Richard Zeckhauser. 1966. "An Economic Theory of Alliances." *The Review of Economics and Statistics* 48 (3): 266–279.

Oneal, John. 1990. "The Theory of Collective Action and Burden Sharing in NATO." *International Organization* 44 (3): 379–402.

Onuf, Nicholas. 1989. *A World of Our Making: Rules and Rule in Social Theory and International Relations.* Columbia, S.C.: University of South Carolina Press.

———. 1994. "The Constitution of International Society." *European Journal of International Law* 5 (1): 1–19.

———. 1997a. "A Constructivist Manifesto." In *Constituting International Political Economy,* edited by Kurt Burch and Robert Denemark, 7–17. Boulder: Lynne Rienner.

———. 1997b. "Hegemony's Hegemony in IPE." In *Constituting International Political Economy,* edited by Kurt Burch and Robert Denemark, 91–110. Boulder: Lynne Rienner.

———. 1998. "Constructivism: A User's Manual." In *International Relations in a Constructed World*, edited by Vendulka Kubálková, Nicholas Onuf, and Paul Kowert, 58–78. Armonk, N.Y.: M.E. Sharpe.

Ostrom, Elinor, Roy Gardner, and James Walker. 1994. *Rules, Games, and Common-Pool Resources*. Ann Arbor: University of Michigan Press.

Papandreou, George A. 2000. "A Total Balkan Approach." *Seton Hall Journal of Diplomacy and International Relations* 1: 75–77.

Pecorino, Paul. 1999. "The Effect of Group Size on Public Good Provision in a Repeated Game Setting." *Journal of Public Economics* 72 (1): 121–134.

Pecorino, Paul and Akram Temimi. 2007. "Lotteries, Group Size and Public Good Provision." *Journal of Public Economic Theory* 9 (3): 451–465.

———. 2008. "The Group-Size Paradox Revisited." *Journal of Public Economic Theory* 10 (5): 785–799.

Perc, Matjaž, and Attila Szolnoki. 2010. "Coevolutionary Games—a Mini Review." *Biosystems*. 99: 109–125.

Pilisuk, Mark and Jennifer Achord Roundtree. 2008. *Who Benefits from Global Violence and War: Uncovering a Destructive System*. Westport, Conn.: Praeger Security International.

Popper, Karl. 1967. "The Rationality Principle." In *Popper Selections*, edited by David W. Miller, 357–365. Princeton, N.J.: Princeton University Press.

Pouliot, Vincent. 2008. "The Logic of Practicality: A Theory of Practice of Security Communities." *International Organization* 62 (2): 257–288.

Pouliot, Vincent and Jérémie Cornut. 2015. "Practice Theory and the Study of Diplomacy: A Research Agenda." *Cooperation and Conflict* 50 (3): 297–315.

Qian, Nancy and David Yanagizawa. 2009. "The Strategic Determinants of U.S. Human Rights Reporting: Evidence from the Cold War." *Journal of the European Economic Association* 7 (2/3): 446–457.

Radio Renascenca. 1999. "Portugal Puts Planes on Alert for NATO Strikes on Serbia. Radio Interview with Portuguese Defense Minister Veiga Simao, January 20, 1999." *BBC Monitoring International Reports*. Retrieved from http://nl.newsbank.com on February 25, 2018.

Rapoport, Anatol and Melvin Guyer. 1966. "A Taxonomy of 2 x 2 Games." *General Systems* 11: 203–214.

Reich, Simon and Richard Ned Lebow. 2014. *Good-Bye Hegemony! Power and Influence in the Global System*. Kindle edition. Princeton, N.J.: Princeton University Press.

Risse, Thomas. 2000. "'Let's Argue!' Communicative Action in World Politics." *International Organization* 54 (1): 1–39.

Risse, Thomas and Kathryn Sikkink. 1999. "The Socialization of International Human Rights Norms into Domestic Practices: Introduction." In *The Power of Human Rights: International Norms and Domestic Change*, edited by Thomas Risse, Stephen C. Ropp, and Kathryn Sikkink, 1–38. Cambridge: Cambridge University Press.

Roberts, James C. 1997. "The Rational Constitution of Agents and Structures." In *Constituting International Political Economy*, edited by Kurt Burch and Robert A. Denemark, 155–168. Boulder, Colo.: Lynne Rienner.

———. 2017. "What Do Rules do? Making Room for Rationality in Constructivist Thought." in *The Art of World-Making: Nicholas Greenwood Onuf and his Critics*, edited by Harry D. Gould, 80–90. New York: Routledge.

Roosevelt, Eleanor. 1948. "The Struggle for Human Rights." Speech given at the Sorbonne, Paris, Sept. 28, 1948. Accessed on February 6, 2010 through *The Eleanor Roosevelt Papers Project*, George Washington University, http://www.gwu.edu/~erpapers/documents/speeches/doc026617.cfm.

Rozin, Paul and Deborah Schiller. 1980. "The Nature and Acquisition of a Preference for Chili Pepper by Humans." *Motivation and Emotion* 4 (7): 77–101.

Ruben, David-Hillel. 1990. *Explaining Explanation.* New York: Routledge.

Runge, Carlisle, F. 1984. "Institutions and the Free Rider: The Assurance Problem in Collective Action." *The Journal of Politics* 46 (1): 154–181.

Sallot, Jeff. 1999. "Canada's Tone Turning Dovish. Ministers Give Up Talk of Ground War." *The Globe and Mail.* Toronto, May 20, 1999, page A16.

Samuelson, Paul A. 1938. "A Note on the Pure Theory of Consumer's Behavior." *Economica*, New Series 5 (17): 61–71.

———. 1954. "The Pure Theory of Public Expenditure." *Review of Economics and Statistics* 36 (4): 387–389.

———. 1955. "Diagrammatic Representation of a Theory of Public Expenditure." *Review of Economics and Statistics* 37 (4): 350–356.

Sandler, Todd. 1992. *Collective Action: Theory and Applications.* Ann Arbor: University of Michigan Press.

———. 1993. "The Economic Theory of Alliances: A Survey." *The Journal of Conflict Resolution* 37 (3): 446–483.

———. 1998. Global and Regional Public Goods: A Prognosis for Collective Action. *Fiscal Studies* 19 (3): 221–247.

———. 2004. *Global Collective Action.* New York: Cambridge University Press.

———. 2006. "Regional Public Goods and International Organizations." *Review of International Organizations* 1 (1): 5–25.

———. 2015. "Collective Action: Fifty Years Later." *Public Choice* 164 (3/4): 195–216.

Sandler, Todd and John Cauley. 1975. "On the Economic Theory of Alliances." *The Journal of Conflict Resolution* 19 (2): 330–348.

Sandler, Todd and John F. Forbes. 1980. "Burden Sharing, Strategy, and the Design of NATO." *Economic Inquiry* 18 (3): 425–44.

Santos, Francisco C., Marta D. Santos, and Jorge M. Pacheco. 2008. "Social Diversity Promotes the Emergence of Cooperation in Public Goods Games." *Nature* 454 (7201): 213–215.

Schachter, Oscar. 1982. *International Law in Theory and Practice.* Norwell, Mass.: Kluwer Academic Publishers.

Schlesinger, Arthur Jr., 1978. "Human Rights and the American Tradition." *Foreign Affairs* 57 (3): 503–526.

Schofield, Norman. 1977. "Dynamic Games of Collective Action." *Public Choice* 30: 77–105.

Sen, Amartya. 1986. "Behaviour and the Concept of Preference." In *Rational Choice*, edited by Jon Elster, 59–81. New York: New York University Press.

Sending, Ole J. 2002. "Constitution, Choice and Change: Problems with the 'Logic of Appropriateness' and Its Use in Constructivist Theory." *European Journal of International Relations* 8 (4): 443–470.

Shibata, Hirofumi. 1971. "A Bargaining Model of the Pure Theory of Public Expenditure." *Journal of Political Economy* 79 (1): 1–29.

Simon, Jeffrey and Hans Binnendijk. 1997. "Romania and NATO: Membership Reassessment at the July 1997 Summit." *Strategic Forum*. National Defense University Institute for National Strategic Studies. No. 101. Retrieved from https://permanent.access.gpo.gov/lps496/Strforum/sf101/forum101.html on January 5, 2019.

Singhvi, L. M., Rapporteur. 1993. "Report of the Regional Meeting for Asia of the World Conference on Human Rights." United Nations. Document ID: A/CONF.157/ASRM/8-A/CONF.157/PC/59.

Snidal, Duncan. 1985. "The Limits of Hegemonic Stability Theory." *International Organization* 39 (4): 579–614.

Spero, Joan and Jeffrey Hart. 1997. *The Politics of International Economic Relations*. Fifth edition. New York: St. Martins Press.

Spero, Joan and Jeffrey Hart. 2010. *The Politics of International Economic Relations*. Seventh edition. Belmont, Calif.: Wadsworth.

Stigler, George J. 1950a. "The Development of Utility Theory I." *Journal of Political Economy* 58 (4): 307–327.

———. 1950b. "The Development of Utility Theory II." *Journal of Political Economy* 58 (5): 373–396.

Sugden, Robert. 1982. "On the Economics of Philanthropy." *The Economic Journal* 92 (366): 341–350.

Tananbaum, Duane A. 1985. "The Bricker Amendment Controversy: Its Origins and Eisenhower's Role." *Diplomatic History* 9 (1): 73–93.

Taylor, Michael. 1976. *Anarchy and Cooperation*. New York: John Wiley and Sons.

———. 1987. *The Possibility of Cooperation*. Cambridge: Cambridge University Press.

Taylor, M. and H. Ward. 1982. "Chickens, Whales, and Lumpy Goods: Alternative Models of Public-Goods Provision." *Political Studies* 30 (3): 350–370.

Teson, Fernando R. 1985. "International Human Rights and Cultural Relativism." *Virginia Journal of International Law* 25 (4): 869–898.

Tomuschat, Christian. 2010. "International Covenant on Civil and Political Rights (1966). Oxford Public International Law." Retrieved from http://opil.ouplaw.com/view/10.1093/law:epil/9780199231690/law-9780199231690-e835 on April 30, 2018.

Triffin, Robert. 1960. *Gold and the Dollar Crisis: The Future of Convertibility*. New Haven: Yale University Press.

Tsygankov, Andrei P. 2014. "Contested Identity and Foreign Policy: Interpreting Russia's International Choices." *International Studies Perspectives* 15 (1): 19–35.

Tversky, Amos and Daniel Kahneman. 1981. "The Framing of Decisions and the Psychology of Choice." *Science*, New Series 211(4481): 453–458.

United Nations General Assembly (UNGA). 1948. "Draft Universal Declaration of Human Rights: Report of the Third Committee." United Nations Document A/777, A/PV.180, December 9, 1948.

———. 2005. "Resolution Adopted by the General Assembly on 16 September 2005: World Summit Outcome." United Nations Document A/Res/60/1.

———. 2009. "Implementing the Responsibility to Protect: Report of the Secretary-General." United Nations Document A/64/667.

UNHCHR. 2010a. "International Human Rights Law." United Nations Office of the High Commissioner for Human Rights. Retrieved from http://www.ohchr.org/EN/ Professional Interest/Pages/InternationalLaw.aspx on February 11, 2010.

———. 2010b. "The Core International Human Rights Instruments and Their Monitoring Bodies." United Nations Office of the High Commissioner for Human Rights. Retrieved from http://www2.ohchr.org/english/law/index.htm#core on February 11, 2010.

UNHCHR. 1999. "Kosovo Crisis Update." Office of the United Nations High Commissioner on Refugees. Retrieved from http://www.unhcr.org/cgi-bin/texis/vtx/news/opendoc.htm? tbl=NEWS &page=home&id=3ae6b80dc on February 14, 2010.

UN Security Council. 1999. "Transcript of the United Nations Security Council Meeting on March 24, 1999." United Nations Document S/PV.3988.

Urfalino, Philippe. 2014. "The Rule of Non-Opposition: Opening Up: Decision-Making by Consensus." *The Journal of Political Philosophy* 22 (3): 320–341.

U.S. Department of State. 1960. "Foreign Relations of the United States, 1958–1960, Foreign Economic Policy, Volume IV. Document 60: U.S. International Financial and Monetary Policy." Retrieved from history.state.gov/historicaldocuments/frus1958-60v04/comp2 on February 26, 2016.

U.S. Senate. 1952. *Congressional Record.* 82nd Congress. Volume 97, Part 6, 8263.

Wagner, Eric. 2006. "The Peaceable Kingdom? The National Myth of Canadian Peacekeeping and the Cold War." *Canadian Military Journal* (Winter 2006–2007): 45–54.

Wallner, Klaus. 2002. "The Provision of Public Goods in International Relations: A Comment on 'Goods, Games, and Institutions.'" *International Political Science Review* 23 (4): 393–401.

Waltz, Kenneth. 1979. *Theory of International Politics.* New York: Random House.

Wang, Jing, Bin Wu, Xiaojie Chen, and Long Wang. 2010. "Evolutionary Dynamics of Public Goods Games with Diverse Contributions in Finite Populations." *Physical Review E.* 81: 1–8.

Weber, Max. 1978. [1922] *Economy and Society: An Outline of Interpretive Sociology.* Edited by Guenther Roth and Claus Wittich. Translated by Ephraim Fischoff et al. Berkeley: University of California Press.

Weldes, Jutta. 1989. "Marxism and Methodological Individualism: A Critique." *Theory and Society,* 18 (3): 353–386.

Wendt, Alexander E. 1987. "The Agent-Structure Problem in International Relations Theory." *International Organization* 41 (3): 335–370.

———. 1999. *Social Theory of International Relations.* New York: Cambridge University Press.

WGBH. 2014a. "A Kosovo Timeline." *FRONTLINE.* Retrieved from http://www.pbs.org/wgbh/ pages/frontline/shows/kosovo/etc/cron.html, on March 21, 2017.

———. 2014b. "Facts and Figures." *FRONTLINE*. Retrieved from http://www.pbs. org/wgbh/pages/frontline/shows/kosovo/etc/facts.html, on March 26, 2017.

Whitman, Marina v. N. 1975. "Leadership without Hegemony: Our Role in the World Economy." *Foreign Policy* 20 (Autumn): 138–160.

Whitworth, Sandra. 2005. "Militarized Masculinities and the Politics of Peace-keeping: The Canadian Case." In *Critical Security Studies in World Politics*, edited by Ken Booth, 89–109. Boulder, Colo.: Lynne Rienner.

Wight, Colin. 2006. *Agents, Strictures, and International Relations*. Cambridge: Cambridge University Press.

World Gold Council. 2011. "Historical Data - Annual Time Series on World Official Gold Reserves since 1845." Retrieved from www.gold.org/research/historical -data-annual-time-series-world-official-gold-reserves-1845 on March 4, 2016.

Wunderlich, Carmen. 2013. "Theoretical Approaches in Norm Dynamics." In *Norm Dynamics in Multilateral Arms Control: Interests, Conflicts, and Justice*, edited by Harald Müller and Carmen Wunderlich, 20–47. Athens, Ga.: University of Georgia Press.

Wyplosz, Charles. 1999. "International Financial Instability." In *Global Public Goods: International Cooperation in the 21st Century*, edited by Inge Kaul, Isabelle Grunberg, and Marc Stern, 152–189. New York: Oxford University Press.

Zajonc, Robert B. 1980. "Feeling and Thinking: Preferences Need No Inferences." *American Psychologist* 35 (2): 151–175.

Zajonc, Robert B. and Hazel Markus. 1982. "Affective and Cognitive Factors in Preferences." *Journal of Consumer Research* 9 (2): 123–131.

Zimmerman, Hubert. 2002. *Money and Security: Troops, Monetary Policy, and West Germany's Relations with the United States and Britain, 1950–1971*. Cambridge, U.K.: Cambridge University Press.

INDEX

Adenauer, Konrad, 54–55, 62
advocacy, 109
algebraic proofs, 32, 42–47
alliances, 82
altruism, 38
Anderson, Robert, 55, 61–63
Annan, Kofi, 110
anti-Americanism, 78–80
Art, Robert, 71–72
assurance (game), 38–39, *39*
assurance utility model, *39*

balance. *See* stabilization
bandwagon effect, 108, *108*
Bangkok Resolution, 103
Ban Ki-moon, 110
Bank of International Settlements
  (BIS), 55
behavior, 5–6, 17–18, 24, 28, 121;
  appropriate behavior, 108–9; of
  interactions, 40–41, 65
beliefs, 13–14
benefits, 36, 46–47
Bentham, Jeremy, 13–14, 101. *See also*
  utilitarianism
BIS. *See* Bank of International
  Settlements
Bosnia. *See* Yugoslavia
Bretton Woods conference, 51–53, 66n2
Bricker, John W., 117
Bricker Amendment, 117–18
Britain, 50, 57
Bush, George W., 73

Canada, 58, 71, 75, 84, 111; Greece
  and, 124; politics in, 76–78, *77*.
  See also North Atlantic Treaty
  Organization
capitalism, 59
Carol I (king), 89, 91
causal factors, 21–22
Ceaușescu, Nicolae, 93
chicken (game), 38–39, *39*
chicken utility model, *39*
Clark, Wesley, 83
Clinton, Bill, 72–73, 80
club goods, 68–69
Cohen, William, 70
Cold War, 82–83, 87–96, *96*, 116,
  118–19, 123
collateral damage, 52
collective action, 31, 36, 38, 42, 112–13
collective security, 67–69
commodities, 43
communication, 14
communism, 10–11, 58–59
competition, 20–21
consensus, 103–4, 107–8, *108*
constructivism, 1–2, 4–5, 13–19; foreign
  policy in, 7–8, 113; international
  relations in, 21, 125–26
consumption, 2–3, 38, 45
Contact Group, 70, 84n2
contributions, 27–28, 30–31, *31*, 85n7
cooperation, 1–3, 65, 74–75, *75*, 83–84
cost, 35–36, 40, 43, 46–47
Crimean War, 87–88

criticism, 4–5
Croatia, 75. *See also* Yugoslavia
cultural relativism, 102–3, 115–16
Cuza, Alexandru Ioan, 88–89
Cyprus, 80

decisions, 121–26; consensus and, 107;
  by groups, 10, 103–4; individuals
  and, 29–31, *31*, 33–34; information
  and, 114–15; in joint provision,
  45–46; for privileged groups, 40,
  118–19; psychology of, 15, 24;
  stalemates in, 38–39; theorems for,
  42–47; in trade, 25–29
desire, 15, 17, 26, 38
Dillon, C. Douglas, 55, 62–63
disease, 49
divisibility, 2–3

Ebola epidemic, 49
economics: algebraic proofs in, 32,
  42–47; behavior and, 18; Chicken
  (game) in, 38–39, *39*; of club goods,
  68–69; communism, 10–11, 58–59; of
  cooperation, 74–75, *75*; of disease,
  49; flat indifference curves, 37;
  Group of Ten, 63; for groups, 40–41;
  hegemony in, 54; idiosyncratic taste
  in, 16–17; indifference curves in, 35;
  of indivisibility, 2; of international
  relations, 4–5; microeconomics,
  23; Nash equilibriums in, 26, 38,
  78, 81, *81*, 95; of organization, 27;
  psychology and, 14; public goods
  game for, *59–60*, 59–65, *62*, *64*;
  social interaction and, 26; supply
  and demand, 19; symbols for, 41; of
  threshold goods, 83–84; threshold
  goods in, 74–75, *75*; of war, 50–53,
  55–56, 64. *See also* cost; rational
  choice; utilitarianism
Eisenhower, Dwight D., 54–55, 61–62,
  118
empiricism, 121–22, 126n1
epistemology, 10, 14–15, 21–22, 121–26

Europe: Cold War for, 93–96, *96*; Japan
  and, *60*, 60–61, 64; politics in, 78–79,
  96–97
evolutionary games, 29
excludability, 2–3
expected value, 48n4

Federal Republic of Yugoslavia. *See*
  Yugoslavia
financial stability, 49–50, 53–54
flat indifference curves, 37
foreign policy, 3, 7–8, 10–11, 91, 113
Franz Ferdinand (Archduke), 68
Friedman, Milton, 14

game theory, 9–10, 25–26, 28–29, 46;
  indifference curves for, 38–39, *39*;
  for military intervention, 95–96, *96*;
  for no conflict games, 77, 77–78. *See
  also specific games*
GDP. *See* Gross Domestic Product
Gelbard, Robert, 70
globalization: of advocacy, 109; anti-
  Americanism in, 78–79; Bretton
  Woods conference for, 52–53; Cold
  War and, 118–19; of collective
  action, 112–13; collective security
  in, 67–69; cultural relativism in,
  102–3; financial stability in, 53–54;
  hegemony in, 55; history of, 50–51;
  human rights in, 68, 108–14, *114*;
  interactions in, 71–81, 75, *77*, *81*;
  Kosovo in, 97, 124; leadership in,
  110; military intervention in, 69–71,
  94–95; multilateralism in, 55–56;
  nationalism in, 53; NATO in, 85n5;
  norm development in, 111–13,
  118–19; politics of, 58–59, 83–84;
  relationships in, 80; of religion,
  87–88; strategy in, 57; of trade, 65;
  UN in, 76–77; of war, 62–63, 89–90.
  See also international relations
global monetary system, 66n1; in
  international relations, 52–57;
  leadership and, 49–52; for U.S.,
  57–65, *59–60*, *62*, *64*

gold-exchange standard, 50, 54–55, 61
Greece: Canada and, 124; identity for, 71, 78–81, *81*; preferences for, 75, 84, 85n6. *See also* North Atlantic Treaty Organization
Gross Domestic Product (GDP), 51, 123
Group of Ten, 63, 66n3
groups: Contact Group, 70, 84n2; decisions by, 10, 103–4; economics for, 40–41; interactions in, 40; latent groups, 36–37, 48n11; *The Logic of Collective Action* (Olson), 25; neuroscience of, 16–17; ontology of, 6–7; preferences for, 57–58; prisoner's dilemma (game), 9; privileged groups, 34, 40, 81, *81*, 118–19; psychology of, 25; resources and, 34; rules for, 17–18; size of, 27–28; special preferences for, 74–75; supply and demand for, 30–31; technology for, 28; theory for, 3–4, 7–8; in utilitarianism, 26–27

hegemony, 54–57, 66n1
Herodotus, 87
history: of analysis, 1; Bangkok Resolution, 103; of globalization, 50–51; of gold-exchange standard, 54–55, 61; of human rights, 99–104; IBRD, 53; of NATO, 67–69, 84n4; of peacekeeping missions, 76; Račak massacre, 70; of Romania, 87–93; of UN, 105; of Yugoslavia, 84n1, 90–93
Holbrooke, Richard, 72
human rights, 124–25; in globalization, 68, 108–14, *114*; history of, 99–104; policy for, 104–8, *108*; psychology of, 114–19; Račak massacre, 70; utilitarianism and, 11; in Yugoslavia, 67–69
Humphrey, John P., 105–6

IBRD. *See* International Bank for Reconstruction and Development
identity, 121–26; for Canada, 71, 75–76, 84; for Greece, 71, 78–81,

81; individual identity, 20, 40–41; in international relations, 56; nationalism and, 72–73, 87–93, 96–97; for NATO, 71–81, 75, *77*, *81*; projected identity, 8; psychology of, 7–8, 17, 24, 96–97; reputation and, 109; social identity, 20; from social interaction, 18–19; tastes and, 20–21; for U.S., 65
idiosyncratic taste, 16–17
IMF. *See* International Monetary Fund
indifference analysis, 48n6
indifference curves, 35, 37–39, *39*, 59, *59*
individuals: behavior of, 121; collective action for, 42; commodities for, 43; consensus for, 108; contributions for, 30–31, *31*; cost for, 43, 47; decisions and, 29–31, *31*, 33–34; expected value for, 48n4; individual identity, 20, 40–41; optimal allocation for, 44; preferences and, 40–41, 47n3; private goods for, 47n2; psychology of, 40; utilitarianism for, 37–38, 48n7
indivisibility, 2, 11n1
information, 114–15
interactions, 28; behavior of, 40–41, 65; in globalization, 71–81, *75*, *77*, 81; social interaction, 2, 4, 18–19, 26, 110
intermediate utility model, *36*
internalization, 112–13
International Bank for Reconstruction and Development (IBRD), 53
International Monetary Fund (IMF), 51–53, 63
international relations: Bretton Woods conference for, 51; collateral damage in, 52; in constructivism, 21, 125–26; cooperation in, 1–3, 83–84; economics of, 4–5; global monetary system in, 52–57; identity in, 56; policy for, 67–68; psychology of, 6–8; rational choice and, 3–4; scholarship on, 71–72; stabilization

in, 34; success in, 8–11. *See also*
   trade
international socialization, 110

Japan, *60,* 60–61, 64
Johnson, Lyndon B., 61
joint provision, 45–46, 47

Keynes, John Maynard, 51, 66n2
Kosovo, 93–97, *96,* 124. *See also*
   Yugoslavia

latent groups, 36–37, 48n11
latent indifference curves, 59, *59*
latent utility model, *37*
leadership, 49–52, 52–57, 71–72, 93–94,
   110
Libya, 114–15
The Logic of Collective Action (Olson),
   3–4, 25
Lukes, Steven, 102

Macedonia, 78. *See also* Yugoslavia
MacIntyre, Alistair, 101–2
management policies, 61
Mason, Paul D., 75–76
McCain, John, 73–74
Medvedev, Dmitri, 8
Michael (king), 91
microeconomics, 23
military intervention: for Canada,
   111; game theory for, 95–96, *96;* in
   globalization, 69–71, 94–95; politics
   of, 67–69; psychology of, 73–74,
   78–81, *81;* scholarship on, 80, 82. *See
   also* war
Milosevic, Slobodan, 69–71, 73–74, 77
models, 122–25; assurance utility
   model, *39;* chicken utility model,
   39; for collective action, 31; for
   contributions, 27; from game
   theory, 25–26; intermediate utility
   model, *36;* latent utility model,
   37; for privileged groups, 34;
   privileged utility model, *35;* for
   rational choice, 23–24; science of,
   22–23; special privileged utility

model, *33,* 48n9, 59–60, *59–60;* for
   utilitarianism, 30, 32–33, *33,* 48n8,
   57–58, 104–5, 126n2
Montenegro, 84n1. *See also* Yugoslavia
Morsink, Johannes, 105
motivation, 15, 50
multilateralism, 55–56

Nash equilibriums, 26, 38, 78, 81, *81,*
   95
nationalism: GDP in, 51; in
   globalization, 53; identity and,
   72–73, 87–93, 96–97; leadership and,
   52–57; policy for, 57–58; preferences
   and, 61–62, *62,* 65; Yugoslavia and,
   82–84
National Salvation Front (NSF), 93
NATO. *See* North Atlantic Treaty
   Organization
neorealism, 20–21
neuroscience, 16–17
Nickel, James, 102
Nixon, Richard M., 58
no conflict games, *77,* 77–78
nomological law, 13, 121–22
non-excludability, 2, 3, 49, 50, 82, 110
norm development, 111–13, 118–19
North Atlantic Treaty Organization
   (NATO), 85n5, 85n7; Cold War for,
   82–83, 123; history of, 67–69, 84n4;
   Libya for, 114–15; policy for, 92–97,
   96; preferences for, 71–81, *75, 77, 81;*
   in Yugoslavia, 69–71
n-person game, 27–28
NSF. *See* National Salvation Front

Olson, Mancur, 3–4, 25, 34
Onuf, Nicholas, 1, 19, 24
ontology, of groups, 6–7
optimal allocation, 44
organization, 27
Ottoman Empire, 88
Owen, David, 73–74

parallel typologies, 48n11
Pareto efficiency, 26
Pareto Optimal equilibrium, 95–96, *96*

peacekeeping missions, 76
philosophy, 99–102, 110–16, *114*, 121–22, 126n1
policy: from Cold War, 82–83, 116; for communism, 58–59; foreign policy, 3, 7–8, 10–11, 91, 113; for human rights, 104–8, *108*; for IMF, 53, 63; for international relations, 67–68; management policies, 61; for nationalism, 57–58; for NATO, 92–97, *96*; R2P, 110–14, *114*; in U.S., 117
politics: in Canada, 76–78, *77*; of communism, 10–11; in Europe, 78–79, 96–97; of globalization, 58–59, 83–84; of military intervention, 67–69; psychology of, 8; of religion, 69–71; of slavery, 100–101; theory of, 22–23; Universal Declaration of Human Rights, 99–107, 112, 115, 117–18, 124–25; in U.S., 52–57
preferences, 19; in game theory, 46; for Greece, 75, 84, 85n6; for groups, 57–58; individual identity and, 40–41; individuals and, 40–41, 47n3; nationalism and, 61–62, *62*, 65; for NATO, 71–81, 75, *77*, *81*; in prisoner's dilemma (game), *35*, 35–36; for privileged groups, 81, *81*; special preferences, 73–75; in trade, *32–33*, 32–38, *35–37*; 2X2 variable sum game for, *32–33*, 32–35. *See also* tastes
prisoner's dilemma (game), 9, 29; preferences in, *35*, 35–36; psychology from, 26–27; stabilization in, *64*, 64–65
private goods, 31, 47n2
privileged groups, 34, 40, 81, *81*, 118–19
privileged utility model, *35*
projected identity, 8
psychology: appropriate behavior in, 108–9; of assurance, 38–39, *39*; bandwagon effect, 108, *108*; behavior and, 5–6; of beliefs,

13–14; of causal factors, 21–22; of consensus, 103–4; of constructivism, 4–5, 18; of consumers, 2–3; of cooperation, 65; of decisions, 15, 24; economics and, 14; of financial stability, 49–50; of groups, 25; of hegemony, 54; of human rights, 114–19; of identity, 7–8, 17, 24, 96–97; of individuals, 40; internalization, 112–13; of international relations, 6–8; of latent groups, 36–37; of military intervention, 73–74, 78–81, *81*; neuroscience and, 16; nomological law and, 121–22; in n-person game, 27–28; of politics, 8; from prisoner's dilemma (game), 26–27; of private goods, 31; public bad, 11, 49–52 68, 114–19, 125; of social interaction, 2, 4; of socialization, 20–21; of sole provision, 43; of trade, 125–26; of utilitarianism, 6–7
public bad, 11, 49–52, 68, 114–19, 125
public goods. *See* international relations; trade
public goods game, *59–60*, 59–65, *62*, *64*

R2P. *See* Responsibility to Protect
Račak massacre, 70
rational choice: criticism of, 4–5; epistemology of, 10, 14–15, 121–26; international relations and, 3–4; microeconomics and, 23; models for, 23–24; Pareto Optimal equilibrium, 95–96, *96*; socially constructed tastes and, 6–8; supply and demand in, 19; utilitarianism and, 13–19
relationships, 50, 67–69, 80
religion, 67–71, 87–88
reputation, 109
resources, 34
Responsibility to Protect (R2P), 110–14, *114*
Romania, 10–11, 87–96
Roosevelt, Eleanor, 99, 115

rules, 17–18, 24
Russia, 87–93, 106. *See also* Cold War;
    Yugoslavia
Rwanda, 110

Santa Cruz, Hernan, 106–7
Saudi Arabia, 104–5
scholarship, 9–10, 40–41, 71–72, 80, 82
science, 16–17, 21–23
SDRs. *See* Special Drawing Rights
Serbia, 79, 89. *See also* Yugoslavia
Simitis, Costas, 78–79
slavery, 100–101
social capital, 15
social cost, 51–52
social interaction, 2, 4, 18–19, 26, 110
socialization, 20–21
socially constructed tastes, 6–8
sole provision, 43, 44
Soviet Union. *See* Cold War; Russia
Special Drawing Rights (SDRs), 63
special preferences, 73–75
special privileged utility model, *33*,
    48n9, 59–60, *59–60*
stabilization: financial stability, 49–50,
    53–54; hegemony for, 56–57; in
    international relations, 34; in
    prisoner's dilemma (game), *64*,
    64–65; for U.S., 52; war and, 58–59
stalemates, 38–39
strategy, 29, 57
substitution, 38, 45
success, 8–11
suppliers, 50
supply and demand, 19, 30–31, 35–36,
    43
symmetry thesis, 121

tastes: in constructivism, 13–19;
    identity and, 20–21; idiosyncratic
    taste, 16–17; socially constructed
    tastes, 6–8; in utilitarianism, 21–24
technology, 28
theory, 9–10, 21n1; of alliances, 82; of
    altruism, 38; for constructivism,
    1–2; for groups, 3–4, 7–8; for
    hegemony, 56–57; of neorealism,

20–21; of nomological law, 13; of
    politics, 22–23; of public bad, 11,
    49–52, 68, 114–19, 125; symmetry
    thesis, 121; theorems, *32*, 42–47; for
    utilitarianism, 21n1. *See also* game
    theory; specific theories
threshold goods, 74–75, *75*, 83–84
trade: communication in, 14;
    competition in, 20–21; decisions
    in, 25–29; foreign policy and, 3, 91;
    globalization of, 65; preferences in,
    32–33, 32–38, *35–37*; psychology
    of, 125–26; relationships in, 50;
    scholarship on, 40–41; for U.S., 51
*Treatise on Tolerance on the Occasion of
    the Death of Jean Calas* (Voltaire), 100
Treaty of Paris, 90
Triffin Dilemma, 54
Turkey, 79, 82–83
2x2 variable sum game, *32–33*, *32–35*,
    122

United Nations (UN), 76–77; history
    of, 105; Universal Declaration of
    Human Rights, 99–107, 112, 115,
    117–18, 124–25. *See also* human
    rights
United States (U.S.): anti-
    Americanism, 78–79; Britain and,
    57; Canada and, 58; GDP in, 123;
    global monetary system for, 57–65,
    59–60, *62*, *64*; gold-exchange
    standard for, 50; identity for, 65;
    in leadership, 71–72; philosophy
    in, 99; policy in, 117; politics in,
    52–57; stabilization for, 52; trade
    for, 51; utilitarianism in, 10. *See also*
    Cold War; North Atlantic Treaty
    Organization
Universal Declaration of Human
    Rights, 99–107, 112, 115, 117–18,
    124–25
U.S. *See* United States
utilitarianism, 5–6, 121–26; assurance
    utility model, *39*; chicken utility
    model, *39*; cost in, 40; desire in, 26;
    groups in, 26–27; human rights and,

11; for individuals, 37–38, 48n7; intermediate utility model, *36*; latent utility model, *37*; models for, 30, 32–33, *33*, 48n8, 57–58, 104–5, 126n2; norm development in, 113–14, *114*; privileged utility model, *35*; psychology of, 6–7; rational choice and, 13–19; sole provision in, 44; special preferences in, 73; special privileged utility model, *33*, 48n9, 59–60, *59–60*; supply and demand in, 43; tastes in, 21–24; theory for, 21n1; in U.S., 10

Voltaire, 100

war: Cold War, 82–83, 87–96, *96*, 116, 118–19, 123; economics of, 50–53, 55–56, 64; globalization of, 62–63, 89–90; stabilization and, 58–59; in Yugoslavia, 71–81
Warsaw Pact, 93
West Africa, 49
World Bank, 51

Yugoslavia: history of, 84n1, 90–93; human rights in, 67–69; leadership in, 93–94; nationalism and, 82–84; NATO in, 69–71; war in, 71–81

About the Author

James C. Roberts is a professor of political science at Towson University where he served as the chairperson of the Department of Political Science and the director of the International Studies Program for many years. His research interests include constructivism, rational choice theory, international political economy, the formation of national identities, and international relations theory. He also worked for many years for the U.S. government conducting evaluations of economic development programs. He received his Ph.D. and Master's degrees from the School of International Service at American University.

www.ingramcontent.com/pod-product-compliance
Lightning Source LLC
Chambersburg PA
CBHW050611280326
41932CB00016B/3000